Laura Alexandrine Smith

Through Romany Songland

Laura Alexandrine Smith

Through Romany Songland

ISBN/EAN: 9783337021481

Printed in Europe, USA, Canada, Australia, Japan

Cover: Foto ©Thomas Meinert / pixelio.de

More available books at **www.hansebooks.com**

THROUGH ROMANY SONGLAND

BY

LAURA ALEXANDRINE SMITH

Authoress of "THE MUSIC OF THE WATERS."

"Only in the Land of Dreams is Freedom,
Only blooms the beautiful in Song."

"In ancient Germany there was a town known by the name of *Singone*, and referred to by Ptolemy; it is believed that in all probability our English word "sing," in Dutch "zingen," and its various forms in other languages, were derived from the habit of singing of the gypsies."
—HENRY KILGOUR.

London
DAVID STOTT, 370, OXFORD STREET, W.
1889

CONTENTS.

	PAGE
Gypsy Song	ix
Introduction	xi
Magyar or Hungarian Gypsy Songs; or, Songs of the Tzigani	1
Songs of the Gitanos or Spanish Gypsies	47
Russian Romany Songs; or, Songs of the Tziggani	89
Anglo-Romany Songs	107
Scotch Gypsy or Tinkler Songs	157
Songs of the Bohémiens; or, French Gypsy Songs	181
The Zigeŭner or Gypsies of the Vaterland	205
Indian Gypsy Songs and Dance Tunes	211
Finale	225

You ask, what is the gypsy life?
Hark, then, and I will tell:

GYPSY SONG.

GYPSY SONG.

. . . Tra la . . . . Tra la a la.

" Hola, hola, hola, hola, some day I'm sure to die,
Hola, hola, hola, hola, and not a soul will sigh ;
Hola, hola, hola, hola, the only boon I crave—
That 'neath the waving greenwood tree
You'll find for me a grave ;
Then at night who can say but my spirit may roam
Through the glade in the shade where I once had a home."

—*Cecil Traherne.*

INTRODUCTION.

PERSECUTED and maligned as the race of Gypsies has ever been, it has yet been able to invoke and retain an amount of interest that more favoured people have failed to attract. In the case of a few brave champions of the Romany cause, this interest may be said to have developed into a life's devotion, and one can scarcely mention the name of Gypsy without our thoughts reverting to such men as George Borrow, C. G. Leland, George Smith of Coalville, and others, who have been pioneers in the attempt at Gypsy redemption. So much has been written on the subject of the origin of these wandering people, known in almost every clime, so many attempts have been made to trace the source of their language, customs, and characteristics, that it is quite unnecessary for me to touch upon either. The researches I have made into Romany history have had but one object in view, namely, the collecting of any specimens of

Romany song that I could find; these researches and their results I now offer, in the hope that they may add one more link to the short chain of sympathy that exists between the lords of the land and the outcast Bohemians, who may be truly termed the vagrants of every country, whose only resting-place is the green earth, whose roof is the broad heaven, and whose house is the tent "they fold like the Arab, and as silently steal away."

Chorley, that eminent authority on national music, is evidently not an enthusiast on that of the Gypsies. He says, "Gypsy music is of very limited value, if disconnected from the Gypsy performance of it, and from the impression made by it on those who, for the sake of sensation, will endure and relish anything, no matter how eccentric it be. Comparatively few Gypsy tunes, save a Russian or Hungarian dance or two, which possibly own some such parentage, have passed into the world's store of melody."

Schubert and Liszt perhaps alone of the great maestros have given us in their works true samples of Romany harmony. In the "Rhapsodies Hongroises" of the latter we are carried away by the Magyar wildness and impetuous passion that have become synonymous with Hungarian music, and if Hungarian then Romany, since the principal elements in Transylvanian melody are of Gypsy origin. Mr. Leland, in his article on Russian Gypsies,* says, " I listened to the strangest, wildest, and sweetest singing I have ever heard. The singing of Lorelies, of syrens, of witches. First one damsel with an exquisite, clear, firm voice began to sing a verse of a love ballad; and as it approached the end, the chorus stole in softly and unperceived, but with exquisite skill, until in a few seconds the summer breeze, murmuring melody over a rippling lake, seemed changed to a midnight tempest roaring over a stormy sea, in which the basso of the black captain pealed like thunder; and, as it died away, a second girl took up the melody very sweetly but with a little more excitement,—it was like a gleam of moonlight on the still agitated waters,—a strange contralto witch-gleam, and then again the water's chorus and the storm, and then another solo yet sweeter, sadder, and stranger,—the movement continually increasing, until all was fast and wild, and mad,—a locomotive quick-step and then a sudden silence—sunlight—the storm had

* *Macmillan's Magazine*, vol. xli.

blown away," and, he adds, "I could only think of those strange fits of excitement which thrill the Red Indian, and make him burst into song."

The sequence I have adopted in the compilation of this little work is due solely to the immeasurable superiority of the music of the Russian, Hungarian, Transylvanian, Italian, and Spanish Gypsies over that of those to be found in England and Scotland, America and France. The Bohemians of this latter country, unlike the Troubadours and Provençal Minstrels who have gained such a reputation for song in the sunny land of France, have no special attainments of a musical sort, whilst the Zigeŭner, or the Romanies, who wander over the German Vaterland, scarcely take the rank in the world of harmony that one would expect, even in the vagrants of the cradle-land of Beethoven, Mozart, and Handel. True, in the Gypseries which are to be found in the neighbourhood of the English Metropolis, or, as the Gypsies call it, "Mi-Krauliskey gav," or, "Royal Town," one may occasionally hear snatches of Romany song ; the men occupied in their favourite trade, namely, "chinning the cost," sometimes enliven the monotony of it by chanting the following verse, perhaps in terseness and expressiveness equal to anything in the whole circle of Gentile poetry.

ROMANY VERSION
OF
GYPSIES' WHITTLING SONG.

"Can you rokra Romany?
Can you play the bosh?
Can you jal adrey the staripan?
Can you chin the cost?"

ENGLISH TRANSLATION.

"Can you speak the Roman tongue?
Can you play the fiddle?
Can you eat the prison loaf?
Can you cut and whittle?"

But for the beauties so characteristic of Gypsy music we must go to the Zingari, Chingali, and Tzigani.

That there is a freemasonry existing amongst the Gypsies scattered over the world, and a cosmopolitanism in the Romany tongue, whether heard on Wandsworth Common, on the Steppes of the Kingdom of the Czar, or in the Valleys of the

Transvaal, is very apparent, since it is possible for a Hungarian Gypsy soldier and an Italian Zingara to understand each other, if not perfectly, at least intelligently.

As professional musicians we meet with the Gypsies in most European countries, generally in small bands, roving from place to place, and entertaining the people with the national melodies of the country. Thus we find them everywhere, especially in Spain, in Russia, in Hungary, Transylvania, Wallachia, and even in South America. In the northern part of Russia they excel as vocal performers; in the Ukraine, in the Danubian Principalities, and in Hungary they are almost exclusively instrumentalists. It cannot exactly be said that they have preserved anywhere a national music of their own. They have adopted in every country the music of the people among whom they live. Still, there is much in their performances which they appear to have traditionally preserved from their Asiatic forefathers. It is impossible to convey by words an accurate idea of the peculiarities of instrumental music so strange and spirited as that of the Gypsies. Some of its characteristics are a strongly marked and effective rhythm, the frequent employment of *superfluous seconds*, and the introduction of various kinds of embellishments. When the Gypsies in Hungary perform a favourite national melody, it becomes a *variation*, or rather, a *fantasia*, founded upon the simple tune. The introduced passages, *graces, turns, shakes, appogiaturas*, are, however, frequently so original, tasteful, and effective that these peculiar performances have obtained a well-merited renown. The same mode of treating a melody in extempore performances prevails in Hindostan, the original home of the Gypsies.

One of our best known authoresses has said, " There is always song somewhere. As the wine-waggon creaks down the hill, the waggoner will chant to the corn that grows upon either side of him. As the miller's mules cross the bridge, the lad, as he cracks his whip, will hum to the blowing alders. In the red clover, the labourers will whet their scythes to a trick of melody. In the quiet evenings, a *Kyrie Eleison* will rise from the thick leaves that hide a village chapel. On the hills the goatherd, high in air amongst the arbutus branches, will scatter on the lonely mountain side stanzas of purest rhythm. By the seashore where Shelley died, the fisherman, rough, and salt, and weather-worn, will string notes of sweetest measure under the tamarisk-tree on his mandoline. But the poetry and music afloat on the air, like the leaves of roses that blossom in a solitude, and drift away to die upon the breeze; there is no one to notice the fragrance, there is no one to gather the leaves." If the waggoner, the mule-driver, the labourer, the goatherd, and the fisherman all find an impetus for their work in chants and occasional bursts of melody, we may be sure we shall not find the Gitana tripping to her contraband profession, namely, that of fortune-telling, with songless lips, nor the Hungarian Gypsy at his trade, principally that of a smith, driving his heavy hammer unaccompanied by some song; nor should we recognize the mirth-loving, rich-coloured Zingara of the Campagna without her mandoline or tambourine.

Human in its sadness, twice human in its eloquence; now sighing as the *Miserere* from a cathedral at midnight; now flooded with the glory of a perfect day in June,—sometimes grand, sometimes simple; now poured from the lark-like throat of some Gypsy maid; now wooed from the tender strings of the violin,—often wild, always passionate, Gypsy music may safely be classed amongst the most interesting and diversified that is to be heard. We may go to the harvesters for choruses, whose regularity admits of no criticism, and whose beauty is apparent in every note, in every phrase; we may listen to the strains of the peasants of Tuscany, or the bead-stringers of Venice, and stand transfixed as some more than usually lovely *stradella* is wafted to us over the lagoons on a still, starry night; but we must go to the Romany tents if we want to hear the real, true, wild songs of the plain and forest, and we must sup with Gypsy minstrels and share the Gypsy shelter to learn the mystery and the meaning of that science which, more than poetry, more than genius of all kinds, is a sublime instinct.

MAGYAR OR HUNGARIAN GYPSY SONGS:

OR,

SONGS OF THE TZIGANI.

"Que ce soit une nation de parias qu'importe à l'art."—LISZT.

" If the earth be God's crown,
Our country is its fairest jewel."
—ALEXANDER PETÖLFI.

MAGYAR OR HUNGARIAN GYPSY SONGS.

THE gypsies having no religion, no taste for politics, and being averse to a military life, have not distinguished themselves in any of these departments. They are, however, excellent musicians, especially those in the east of Europe. In Russia the gypsy singers are quite an institution; and in Hungary, Transylvania, and Moldavia they are noted as players on the violin. The names of Barna Mihaly, Czinka, Panna, and Bihari are known all over Hungary. Barna Mihaly lived, in 1737, in Illesfalva in the Zips Country, and became Court violinist to Cardinal Count Emmerich Csaky. The Cardinal had a full-length portrait of him painted, with the pretty compliment contained in the words " Magyar Orpheus " inscribed on it. The names Sucecawâ, Anzheluzzâ, and Barba are familiar as household words all over Moldavia and Wallachia. Dr. Clarke was of opinion that the national Russian dance, called "Barina," is of gypsy origin, and that our common hornpipe may have been derived from it. The gypsies of Hungary do not usually play by ear only, and are generally led by an

Austrian. Having no national music, they have in every country adopted the music of the inhabitants.

The most important part of the national music of Hungary is thus called because it proceeds from the Magyar portion of the inhabitants. "The so-called Hungarian style of music, as it has come to be recognized, cannot by any means be regarded as indigenous, but may most properly be briefly defined as the product of a commixture of several races. More than one-fourth or perhaps half of the population of Hungary proper (*i.e.*, Transleithan Hungary, as it has come to be called since its union with the Austrian Empire, 1869) consists of Magyars, the descendants of the ancient Scythians of the Tartar-Mongolian stock, who after wandering from the Ural Mountains to the Caspian Sea, and thence to Kiov, established themselves in Hungary in the ninth century. The remainder of the population is made up of Slavs, Germans, Wallachians, Jews, and gypsies. Of this mixed population the Magyars, as the dominant lords of the soil, and the gypsies, as the privileged musicians of the country, are in the main to be regarded as the joint originators of the national style."*

The union of these two latter races resulted in the combination of their musical charts. The chief characteristic of the Magyar music is the peculiarity of its

* *Monthly Musical Record*, for February and March, 1887.

rhythm; and that of the gypsy, the presence of turns, and embellishments, and "grace-notes" added to and built upon the melody, and eventually becoming a most important feature in it. This latter peculiarity, together with the scale, which is characteristic of Hungarian music—a scale with two superfluous seconds, or the harmonic minor with a sharp fourth—

seem to indicate an Asiatic origin (the ordinary European scales are also in use). Three-four time, and consequently six-eight, is unknown in genuine Magyar music, save amongst modern Hungarian composers in slow movements. The turns and embellishments added to the melody are of gypsy, and hence Oriental origin. Hadyn first used gypsy music (see his well-known Gypsy Rondo); Schubert, most of all, has made use of it in his divine compositions; Brahm has worked much of its fantastic element into his celebrated "Ungarische Tänze;" and Joachim, who, like Brahm, is a native of Hungary, occasionally delights his audience with music that if not genuinely Romany is something very nearly akin to it.

A writer in *Temple Bar*, October, 1885, in a very interesting article, entitled "Bivouacking with Hungarian Gypsies," says, *à propos* of gypsy music, that "No festivity ever takes place without the Czigány being summoned to enliven it with his soul-stirring music; he invariably accompanies the Czárdás or national dance, and in some parts of Hungary it is, or, until very recently, was, the custom for a band to attend a funeral procession to the cemetery." A horror of subjection and of labour is the gypsy's ruling passion, and a love of variety in every detail of their strangely wandering life is to be found amongst the Romanies of every land. A gypsy will change his religion quite as often, if not oftener, than his coat. One day Roman Catholic, the next Protestant, it matters little to him where his prayers be said, so long as some savoury stew may follow the grace that heralds its approach. They generally follow the same pursuits in all countries, but in Hungary so many of them are workers in iron that the Hungarians have a proverb which says, "So many gypsies, so many smiths." In no part of the world are gypsies found engaged in the cultivation of the earth, or in the service of a regular master; they are nothing if not thoroughly independent. A gypsy has but one law, and that is his own inclination.

"What care we though we be so small?
The tent shall stand when the palace shall fall,"

is a favourite saying among the Romanies, and they amply verify it. In all lands they are jockeys, thieves, or cheats, and if ever they devote themselves to any toil or trade, it is assuredly in every material point one that comprises some of the necessary characteristics of these callings. " We have found them in the heart of a wild mountain hammering iron, and manufacturing from it instruments either for their own use or that of the neighbouring towns and villages. They may be seen employed in a similar manner in the plains of Russia, or in the bosom of its eternal forests, and whoever inspects the site where a horde of gypsies has encamped in the grassy lines beneath the hazel bushes of merry England, is generally sure to find relics of tin or other metal avouching that they there have been exercising the arts of the tinker or the smith. Perhaps nothing speaks more forcibly for the antiquity of this sect than the tenacity with which they have uniformly preserved their peculiar customs since the period of their becoming generally known ; for unless their habits had become a part of their nature, which could only have been effected by a strict devotion to them through a long succession of generations, it is not to be supposed that after their arrival in civilized Europe they could have retained and cherished them, precisely in the same manner in the various countries where they have found an asylum."*

* From Gerard's "Gypsies."

Liszt, in his volume "Des Bohémiens et de leur Musique en Hongrie," says, "The Magyars have adopted the gypsies as their national mucisians; they have identified themselves with the proud and warlike enthusiasm, with the distressing sadness of the Hungarians, which they know so well how to depict. They have not only associated them with their pleasures and at their banquets, they have wept with their tears in making themselves hearers of their own troubles and trials. The nomadic people, the Tzigani, although spread over many lands, and cultivating elsewhere music, have in no other country been able to give it a value equivalent to that which it has acquired on Hungarian soil, for nowhere else have the gypsies met with, as there, the popular sympathy so necessary to the national aggrandizement of any particular class of song. . . . . Hungary can then, with good right, claim as its own this art of encouraging Romany music, nourished with its corn and with its vines, ripened under its shadow, and with its sun, received with hearty applause, embellished and ennobled, thanks to its protection and to its predilections so closely entwined with its habits and manners, that they are intimately interwoven amongst the dearest souvenirs of every true Hungarian heart."

The Austrian gypsies have many songs which perfectly reflect their character. Most of them are only single verses of a few lines, such as are sung everywhere in Spain; others, which are longer, seem to have grown from the connection of these verses. The following translation from the Roumanian Romany (Vassili Alexandri) gives an idea of their style and spirit :—

GYPSY SONG.

"The wind whistles over the heath,
The moonlight flits over the flood,
And the gypsy lights up his fire
In the darkness of the wood.
   Hurrah!
In the darkness of the wood.

"Free is the bird in the air,
And the fish where the river flows;
Free is the deer in the forest,
And the gypsy wherever he goes.
   Hurrah!
And the gypsy wherever he goes.

  A Gorgio gentleman speaks :—
"Girl, wilt thou live in my home?
I will give thee a sable gown,
And golden coins for a necklace,
If thou wilt be my own."

GYPSY GIRL.

"No wild horse will leave the prairie
For a harness with silver stars,
Nor an eagle the crags of the mountain
For a cage with golden bars.

"Nor the gypsy girl the forest,
Or the meadow, though grey and cold,
For garments made of sable,
Or necklaces of gold."

THE GORGIO.

"Girl, wilt thou live in my dwelling
For pearls and diamonds true?*
I will give thee a bed of scarlet,
And a royal palace too."

GYPSY GIRL.

"My white teeth are my pearlins,
My diamonds my own black eyes,
My bed is the soft green meadows,
My palace the world as it lies."

"Free is the bird in the air,
And the fish where the river flows;
Free is the deer in the forest,
And the gypsy wherever he goes.
                    Hurrah!
And the gypsy wherever he goes."

* "The true or real stone," is the gypsy for a diamond.

The following miserable little song was one discovered by Mr. Leland amongst certain inedited songs of the Transylvanian gypsies in the Kolosvárer dialect :—

> "Na janav ko dad m'ro as,
> Niko mallen mange as,
> Miro gule dai merdyas
> Pirani me pregelyas
> Uva tu o hegedive
> Tu sal mindik pash mauga."

Translation.

> "I've known no father since my birth;
> I have no friend alive on earth;
> My mother's dead this many a day;
> The girl I loved has gone her way.
> Thou violin, with music free,
> Alone art ever true to me."

The two following are well-known Hungarian gypsy songs :—

> "Kis szekeres
> Kis szekeres nagy szekeres,
> Mind megiszsza a mit keres:
> Mig a vásárra oda jar,
> A pénzinek vegire jár."

HUNGARIAN GYPSY TUNE.

"JUHÁSZLEGÉNY SZEGENY."

" Juhászlegény szegeny juhászlegény
Tele pénzzel ez a kövér erszény
Megveszem a szegény séget toled
De rádásul add a szeretödet !
" Ha ez a penzlenne czak foglaló
S meg szaz annyi lenne borravaló
S id adnád a világot rádásnak—
Szeretömet ugysem adnam masnak !"

HUNGARIAN GYPSY TUNE.

The words set to the well-known Racoczy March, I am told, are of gypsy origin; they are as follows:—

WORDS SET TO THE RACOCZY.

"Dyal o pañi repedishes,
M'ro pirano hegedishes.

"Dyal o pañi tale vatra
M'ro pirano klanetalia.

"Dyal o pañi pe kishai
M'ro pirano tsino rai."

Translation.

"The stream runs on with rushing din,
As I hear my true love's violin;

"And the river rolls o'er rock and stone,
As he plays the flute so sweet alone.

"Runs o'er the sand as it began,
Then my true love lives a gentleman."

Leland, describing the inimitable effect of this characteristic composition when he heard it performed by a band of Hungarian gypsies in Paris, says, "As these men played for me, inspired with their own music, feeling and enjoying it far more than the audience, and all because they had got a gypsy gentleman to play to, I appreciated what a life that was to them, and what it should be; not cold-blooded skill, aiming only at excellence or pre-excellence and at setting up the artiste, but a fire and a joy—a selfforgetfulness which whirls the soul away as the soul of the Mœnad went with the stream adown the mountains—*Evoë Bacchus!* This feeling is deep in the heart of the Hungarian gypsy; he plays it; he feels it in every air; he knows the rush of the stream as it bounds onwards—knows that it expresses his deepest desire; and so he has given it words in a song, which to him who has the key is one of the most touching ever written. Yes, music whirling the soul away as on a rushing river, the violin notes falling like ripples, the flute tones all aflow among the rocks; and when it sweeps *adagio* on the sandy bed, then the gypsy player is at heart equal to a lord; then he feels a gentleman. The only true republic is art. There all earthly distinctions pass away; there he is best who lives and feels best, and makes others feel, not that he is cleverer than they, but that he can awaken sympathy and joy. The intense reality of musical art as a comforter to these gypsies of eastern Europe is wonderful."

Mr. Leland's descriptions and quotations on Hungarian gypsy music in his volume "The Gypsies" are so manifold and perfect, that one feels tempted to resort to no other means of attempting to depict the rapturous wildness and fervid sadness of the songs of the Zingari. With him one hears the soul-stirring, madly-exciting, and martial strains of the Rococzy, the almost crazy impetuosity of their beloved Czárdás; the grandeur of the Radetsky Defile; one feels the strains played long ago, the horns of Elfland blowing, and with it all the mingled refrain of wind whistling over a winter city, and the memory of the Romany words, " Kamava tute, miri chelladi."

Mr. C. F. Keary, in an able article on the " Roumanian Peasants and their Songs" (*The Nineteenth Century*, October, 1882), refers several times to the esteem in which gypsy music is held by the people of Roumania, and the want of it in regard to their feelings for its performers. He says, "Greater occasions still are the convivial meetings which take place during the winter months; for, as may be supposed, the months of winter hang heavily on the hands of a people so purely agricultural in their habits. Such a convivial meeting is called a *sedatore* (pronounced *shezetoare*), or *séance*. In these *séances* the gypsies play a considerable part. In Roumania, as in Russia, the gypsy (Tzigan) conducts most of the musical part of the entertainment and dancing. They have a set of instruments peculiar to themselves: the guitar,* the violin,† and a sort of bagpipe called cimpoi; whereas the true Roumanian instruments are the flute‡ and the horn.§ Hence arises the saying that God invented the fluer and the bucium, but the devil invented the cobza, the scripca, and the cimpoi. Thus has the music of Pan its revenge upon the music of Apollo."

The Roumanian of course looks with horror upon the gypsy. He invented a sort of diabolical being called Faraon, who is supposed to be king of the Tzigani; and this name Faraon, which must be the same as Pharaoh, brings us back to the same belief respecting the native country of the people as is expressed in our word gypsy or Egyptian. "Who taught you that song?" was asked of a village girl. "My parents" (ancestors). "And who taught them?" "Faraon. Once they were driving their sheep across a ford, and Faraon appeared and spoke to them."

Mr. Keary gives several specimens of the native village songs, and amongst others a "Gypsy Girl's Lament," which I have taken the liberty of quoting.

---

* Cobza. † Scripca. ‡ Fluer. § Bucium, buccina, or buccinum.

"GYPSY GIRL'S LAMENT."

" 'Swallows, swallows,' little sisters—
Sisters, seek my mother dear;
Tell her from her daughter here
That she send her kirtle red,
For a raven she has wed;
And a large thick veil for shroud,
When the watch-dogs bark aloud.
Her brave dresses, that she take them,
Into one rude bundle make them,
Throw them in the street and burn them—
Utterly to ashes turn them."

There is a Montenegrin legend to the effect that a gypsy forged the nails for the Crucifixion, and that on that account his race has henceforth been accursed of heaven. The gypsies refute this statement and will always tell you that no Romany can tolerate a Jew, because they were the people that murdered our blessed Lord.

The modern Roumanian gypsies are divided into certain classes—*Calderari* (kettle smiths), *Aurari* (gold workers), etc. So exclusively is the smith's a gypsy

and therefore a degrading—craft in Montenegro, that
when in 1872 the Government established an arsenal
at Rieka no natives could be found to fill its well-paid
posts. The gypsies still have a monopoly of iron
working in Roumania; the *Naalband*, or shoeing-smith,
being no smith in our sense at all. He is supplied
with various-sized shoes by the Tzigani, and only
hammers them on.

A writer in *The National Review* for January, 1888,
in an article entitled "A Magyar Musician," quotes
the following remarks from Madame Janka Wohl.
She says, "The Rhapsodies Hongroises bring Hungary
before us under her national, as well as her lyric
aspect; her sufferings, her hopes, her mighty spirit,
all that goes to form the basis of a temperament which
being at the same time supine, heedless, and fantastic,
eludes analysis. . . . The Rhapsodies find an echo
all the world over. . . . But those who have not
heard them played by Lizst himself can form no con-
ception of their true value, or of the magical power
they possess. . . . The fire and the sweetness of
Tokai wine are inherent in those languorous *mélopées*,
in their bold and electric rhythm. . . . The melodies
culled haphazard from the national lyre unroll the
whole scale of its sentiment, meditation, sorrows of
love, sad joys of community, of misfortune, yearnings
of the patriot, a despair which is but another name

for the nostalgia of liberty implanted in the heart of a people who have bled for years in slavery.... Then, by degrees, the rhythm quickens; it becomes sudden, rugged, and abrupt, but is ever of an intoxicating melody.... Gaiety takes the lead, contagious fire thrills the dancers, they seek and flee, they grasp and elude each other; delirium seizes upon the feverish souls that are drawn into the whirlwind of the mad, delicious music.... A delirium which culminates in the wild cry of fury and delight that breaks forth now and again from the lips of the dancer, be he either prince or peasant.... A shrill note of passionate vibration that like the sound of a fanfare electrifies the masses."

Roumanian gypsy women sing their little ones to sleep with soft, sweet, and melodious lullabies, which nearly always begin and end with the slumber-suggesting word *Nani-nani*.

"Nani-nani copilas,
Dormi cu mama, angeras,
Ca mama te-a legana,
Si mama te-a saruta,
Si mamuca ti a canta
Nani-nani, nani-na," etc.

English Version.

"Nani-nani, little treasure,
Sleep, dear angel, near thy mother,
For mother will rock thee,
And mother will clasp thee,
And mother will sing thee
Nani-nani, nani-na," etc.

The refrain of this recalls the Italian verse chanted by the peasant women in some parts of Italy on Christmas Day:—

" Dormi, dormi nel mio seno
Dormi, O, mio fior Nazareno!
Il mio cor sulla sara,
Fa la nina-nana na."

Monsieur Vassili Alexandri has collected many of the ballads and tales of Roumania which existed only amongst the Tzigani. He says, " Les Cigains, les rhapsodes de la Roumanie, allaient d'un endroit à l'autre récitant ou chantant ces poèmes, dont les auteurs sont restés inconnus, qu'aucune main ne s'est jamais occupée de transcrire et qui se sont transmis de bouche en bouche d'une génération à l'autre à travers les siècles." " Tandis que Nicolas Balesco visitait les monastères des Carpathes, cherchant, pour me servir de ses propres paroles, 'sous leurs rimes les traces de la grandeur des ancêtres, Alexandri parcourut à pied les montagnes et les plaines de la Roumanie, recueillant ça et là les traditions et les légendes." (M.A. Ubicini: Introduction, " Ballades et Chants populaires de la Roumanie," recueillés et traduits par V. Alexandri.)

Strange to say, the same day that acquainted me with this most fascinating French book also introduced to my notice Mr. E. C. Grenville Murray's "Doïne; or, The National Songs of Roumania." In his most interesting Introduction, the author says, "The Zingari, who swarm in Moldo-Wallachia, and form a class apart, are the same extraordinary people known to us as gypsies, and who seem to have formed a wandering settlement in almost every country in Europe. There was also, I learn, at one time a distinct race of the Zingari settled in Roumania. They called themselves Netoti, and wandered about the forests little better than petty robbers. They had their chiefs, however, and paid a regular tribute to the Government. They adored the sun and stars, believing in a faith which they are said to have brought from India. [The popular superstition in Moldavia believes that when any one dies his star falls from the heavens, as they believe it first appeared there at his birth and influenced his destiny through life.] In 1831 they were forcibly baptized, and became slaves to the Boyards. The rest of the Zingari formerly lived a roving life, and were spread over the country, divided into Vatachii, or companies. Unheard of horrors were told of them ; for it is the gift of the vulgar to think in the wrong everything and every person they cannot understand. They paid a tax for freedom to their master, who, however, often chose some of them as servants. This race of domestics multiplied rapidly, and becoming Wallach in language and customs forgot the people from whom they sprung. The Zingari are now chiefly employed as musicians, artizans, and miners. They are slaves, and can be bought, sold, and punished with impunity. There are still, however, a company of them who preserve their ancient traditions in almost every village ; and if the traveller chance to be benighted in some peasant's hut, it is there that he will hear the tender Doïne sung, and see a pretty national dance called the 'ora,' which will often remind him of the figures on antique vases. Their dress is notable. They wear full white trousers, a white tunic, and a gay-coloured sash. Their long hair falls in wild disarray beneath their slouched hats, and the long, sweeping moustache gives a marked and chivalrous expression to their splendid faces.

"The women wear their long hair tied in a bunch behind, and falling in a single tress down the back. They wear a long fine white shift embroidered with gay-coloured silks, instead of a gown; this is secured by a red woollen sash, beneath which descends the 'fota,' a kind of embroidered apron reaching to the knees. Their feet are bare; and where, Sir Wanderer have you seen more picturesque figures?

". . . . I think I may venture to believe that I have not deceived myself as to the beauty of the Doïne. Poetry which has stirred the heart of one nation has generally an echo in that of another: for all men have very nearly the same feelings and sympathies, much less modified than we think by distance and custom; 'Le monde est partout comme partout,' said the witty Frenchman; and he was right."

The fate of Ossian, the Songs of the North, the Spanish Ballads, and Romancers would be enough to encourage me to hope for the success of the present work; I need not say that such a hope is altogether apart from that of any success of my own. The Doïne seem, indeed, to me, to have about them something of the character of Ossian, only that instead of belonging to a slow, grave, misty nation like the Scotch, they are the songs of a people who lived beneath a summer sky, and whose dreams were all of sunshine and flowers, of moons and stars, and silver seas.

ROUMANIAN GYPSY AIR.

"Oh! surely melody from heaven was sent,
   To cheer the soul when tired with human strife,
  To soothe the wayward heart by sorrow rent,
    And soften down the rugged road of life."

In an article on Transylvanian Superstitions by Madame Emily de Laszowska Gerard, in *The Nineteenth Century*, July, 1885, there are several allusions made to those of the gypsies. The authoress says, " Transylvania might well be termed the land of superstition, for nowhere else does this curious crooked plant of delusion flourish as persistently and in such bewildering variety. It would almost seem as though the whole species of demons, pixies, witches, and hobgoblins, driven from the rest of Europe by the wand of science, had taken refuge within this mountain rampart, well aware that here they would find secure lurking-places, whence they might defy their persecutors yet awhile. There are many reasons why these fabulous beings should retain an abnormally firm hold on the soil of these parts. . . . . Thirdly, there is the wandering superstition of the gypsy tribes, themselves a race of fortune-tellers and witches, whose ambulating caravans cover the country as with a network, and whose less vagrant members fill up the suburbs of towns and villages. The gypsies take up a different position as regards superstition from either Roumanian or Saxon, since they may be rather considered to be direct causes and mainsprings of superstition, than victims of credulity themselves. The Tzigane, whose religion is of such an extremely superficial nature that he rarely believes in anything as complicated as the immortality of the soul, can hardly be supposed to lay much weight upon the supernatural; and if he instinctively avoids such places as churchyards, gallow-trees, etc., his feelings are rather those of a child who shirks being reminded of anything so unpleasant as death or burial. That, however, these people exercise a considerable influence on their Saxon and Roumanian neighbours is undoubted, and it is a paradoxical fact that the same people who regard the gypsy as an undoubted thief, liar, and cheat in all the common transactions of daily life, do not hesitate to confide in him blindly for charmed medicines and love-potions, and are ready to attribute to him unerring power in deciphering the mysteries of the future. The Saxon peasant will, it is true, often drive away the fortune-teller with blows and curses from his door, but his wife, as often as not, will secretly beckon to her to come in again by the back door, in order to be consulted as to the illness of the cows, or to beg from her a remedy against the fever.

"Wonderful potions and salves, in which the fat of bears, dogs, snakes, and snails, along with the oil of rain-worms, the bodies of spiders and midges rubbed into a paste, and many other similar ingredients, are concocted by these cunning Bohemians, who will sometimes thus make thrice as much money out of the carcass of a dead dog as another from the sale of three healthy pigs. Roumanian and Saxon mothers often believe their infants when sickly to be suffering from the effects of the evil eye; and to undo this spell they will give the child to a gypsy woman to nurse for nine days. Roumania furnishes a remunerative theatre for the fortune-teller's performances, and many old women are to be found in the suburbs of the towns whose dreams of avarice are daily being fulfilled by the credulity of their fellow-creatures. One of the principal trades of the Tzigane is the burning of bricks and tiles, and they are often accused of occasioning lengthy droughts to suit their own purposes. When this has occurred, and the necessary rains have not been produced by soundly beating the guilty Tziganes, the Roumanians sometimes resort to the *Papaluga*, or Rain-Maiden. This is done by stripping a young gypsy girl quite naked and dressing her up with wreaths of flowers and leaves which entirely cover her up, leaving only the head visible. Thus adorned, the *Papaluga* is conducted round the villages in procession, to the sound of music and singing, and every one hastens to water her copiously."

The Wallachian gypsies have many pretty and poetical ideas; for instance, they speak of death as "the betrothed of the world," and jewels they call "tears of the sun." They have a superstition which gives a soul to all flowers; and their idea is that only the sinless

flower is scentless; and so on, the sublime ever blended with the ridiculous. "The little stone of truth rolling through the many ages of the world has gathered and grown grey with the thick mosses of romance and superstition. But tradition must always have that little stone of truth as its kernel. And perhaps he who rejects all is likelier to be wrong than even foolish folk like myself who love to believe all, and who tread the new paths ever thinking of the ancient stories."
—*Ouida.*

In his introduction to his most readable book, " Etudes sur les Tchinghianés ou Bohémiens de l'Empire Ottoman," Monsieur Alexandre Paspati says of the songs of these gypsies, " The wandering musicians know a few songs and legends, intermixed with a number of Turkish and Greek words; the aged amongst the Tchinghianés have assured me that in olden times they sang at the agricultural *fêtes* of the Christians and the Mussulmans many Romany songs, but to-day, owing to the intermarrying of the gypsies with Greek girls, which leads to them speaking more Greek and Turkish than Romany, these have been forgotten, or partly so, since they are not understood. The large number of songs which the Grecian press publishes annually for the use of the people has led to the abolition of the vulgar and insipid tunes of this race. Some few of the songs, in which wine and immorality play the principal parts, have always seemed to me frivolous and wanting in sense and good taste ; but in studying the history of a people one ought to neglect nothing, for even after much labour bestowed on it, the materials for this work are very poor and often very insufficient, and that which to us appears frivolous might be to others very precious information."

Mr. Paspati also gives a very graphic and poetic description of the Eastern gypsy in this same work. He describes them thus :—"In the tents one sees neither papers nor books ; I have never met a gypsy in these parts who knew how to read or write ; never have I seen tears on the face of a Tchinghiané. Their courage during illness is heroic ; they only seek their beds to die, and tearless they bury their dead."

There is no more obstinate set of wanderers than the Tchinghiané. Like the Indians of America, they oppose themselves fiercely to all efforts at civilization, which according to them would "suffocate them." They walk through the town sometimes selling baskets, or iron goods, sometimes leading monkeys and bears ; they see the dress of the townswomen, the cleanliness of the children, the *fêtes* and rejoicings of the people ; but these things make no impression upon them, for them it is all like a dream. At night they return to their tent to enjoy the fruits of their work (such as they are), without ever evincing a desire to mix in the gay life of others. One *fête*, though, the Tchinghianés keep, and that is their *Bakkava*, or the *fête des Chaudrons*. This is held during the spring, when they have left their winter quarters. They all meet on some verdant meadow near the source of a stream. For three days these strange creatures give themselves up to feasting, rejoicing, dancing, and singing. Each gypsy is bound to kill and cook a lamb, of which dainty he is expected to invite all the tribe to partake. The table has to be covered with flowers and to be well provided with wine. Monsieur Paspati says that no evidence of any faith whatever exists amongst the Tchinghianés; not even in their songs and legends, of which some are of very ancient date, is there any religion. "Nothing touches this heart of marble, which laughs at all things, and lives and dies like the beasts."

It seems strange, in the face of this, that a custom so strangely resembling one of the most sacred of all ceremonies should find annual devotees amongst them. The Paschal lamb, and the killing and eating of the same animal at a like season by the Eastern gypsies, almost leads one to believe in a remnant of original faith being still among them. In order to keep up this custom a good deal of pilfering has doubtless first to be gone through—a

Romany never pays for what he can get for nothing; and we may rest assured there is mourning and lamentation in the Turkish farmsteads whilst joy and singing prevail at the *Bakkava:* the cry of many an Ottoman farmer will be

"O where, O where
Has my leetel lamb gone"

in those days set apart by these wanderers as days of feasting and making merry.

The following is a little Roumanian lullaby sometimes heard amongst tent-mothers; it is very popular with the peasant women in some villages:—

LULLABY.—"*NANI-NANI.*"

"Lullaby, my little one,
Thou art mother's darling son;
Loving mother will defend thee,
Mother she will rock and tend thee,
Like a flower of delight,
Or an angel swathed in white.

"Sleep with mother, mother well
Knows the charm for every spell.
Thou shalt be a hero as

Our good lord great Stephen was,
Brave in war and strong in hand,
To protect thy fatherland.

"Sleep, my baby, in thy bed,
God upon thee blessings shed;
Be thou dark and be thine eyes
Bright as stars that gem the skies;
Maiden's love be thine, and sweet
Blossoms spring beneath thy feet."

The two songs which follow are respectively of Transylvanian and East Roumelian origin:—

Vaktri doui kalé iakkai
Miklyom mara goulia dai
Kehaz gulé ta i kalé
Oda manghe kampilé.

Matchin puka mui parno
Kalion dusta la javò
Kehaz parno te gulò
Oda manghe kampilo.

Translation.

For your two black eyes
I left my sweet mother;
Because they were black and sweet
I loved none other.

For your pale little face
I have suffered deeply;
Because it was so pale and fair
I have loved it sweetly.

Vak-tri dou - i ka - lè iakkai miklyom ma-ra goul - ia dai

Ke-haz gou - lè tai - ka-lè O - da man-ghè kam - pi - lè.

Kamalàv tut m'angaliàte
Kasoàv ani dakàr.

Kamalàv te pèravav tut
Veschinde tu o sudrè panènde.

Translation.

I will take you in my arms,
And I will sleep like a king.

I will take you for a walk
Through the forest by the stream.

I believe both these songs are to be found in Adriano Colocci's book on the gypsies, "Gli Zingari."

Dr. Henry Phillips, jun., of Philadelphia, has been kind enough to send me a little volume of Volk-Songs translated from the "Acta Comparations Litterarum Universarum."

I.

Kiss me, dearest darling mine,
And I'll buy a ribbon fine;
Let me nestle on thy arm,
And I'll buy a mentè* warm.
Shouldst thou play a faithless trick
Then I'll get a cudgel thick.

* The fur mantle worn in the Hungarian national costume.

XI.
Forge the iron, strike with might,
Like a true-born gypsy smite;
Yet for all be ever poor,
Full of woe my heart and sore;
Yet should I win a precious aim,
Could I within this glowing frame
My darling's heart till tender smite,
No man was e'er so rich a wight.

XII.
Beauteous is the maiden fair;
Bright her silken robes and rare:
But a gypsy-girl's for me
Far a sweeter sight to see.
In the grass she'll lie so still,
Pet and kiss me all I will.

XIII.
Maid, thy love hath proved my curse,
Stripped me e'en of shirt and purse;
God shall singe thy heart with pain,
Then my own will burst in twain.

XIV.
He's a jolly chap, my beau,
Sure none others like him grow;
In town grey or in fields green,
No one like him can be seen.

When his bow the strings doth sweep,
Great and little, all must weep;
If throughout the world you go—
There's none other like him, no!

In the journal of the Gypsy Lore Society for January, 1889, these three songs were given as being the original settings to some Transylvanian tent-melodies which had been published in the October (1888) number of the same paper. By kind permission of the courteous editor, Mr. David McRitchie, I am enabled to quote these verses and the tunes. I may add that the specimens were supplied, together with a German translation, by Professor Herrmann to the Society. The text and melody of the first were obtained by Alb. Geiger at Marosvásárhely, and were revised by Dr. Herrmann.

" Maru, Devla, kas kames, jaj !
Ke man destul* phabares, man,
Maru, Devla, koka bar, jaj !
Kai nasti chut'ilom pordal."

* Borrowed from the Roumanian.

"Strike whom thou wilt, O God! Alas!
Enough Thy fires have scorched me.
Strike down, O God, this hedge. For ah!
It cannot else surmounted be."

From Anica Čurar, a Wallachian gypsy girl of twenty, imprisoned at Brasso, Kronstadt, in 1886, the music of No. 2 was noted down by the well-known musician Zoltan Heltay; the words written by Dr. Herrmann.

"'De man mol la durul'asa,
Ke me dan tut la brad'asa.'*
Sakade pend'e roma,
Ke has lenge but zŭlta;
Kerel les la čorimasa,
Tai pijel la barimasa."

* Borrowed from the Magyar.

" 'Come, bring a jar of wine to me,
Or I'll the cudgel deal to thee.'
So ever have the gypsies said
When money they in plenty had.
'Twas made by them in penury;
In lofty pride 'twas drunk away."

The third, from a gypsy girl, Maria Prikulič, in the service of Herr Herbst, Cseszora, able to read and write, and sister to the first violin in Belényes, Bihar, her native place.

" Kel'e* caje romani
Sa has mange pirani
Ke gënd'ende,* ke len lan,
Da* me ode na keran.

" Ke vod'i man parä* rän,*
Kana ekha čat† dikhan;
Ke e čaje romani
Sar o salot† lulud'i."

* Borrowed from the Roumanian.
† Borrowed from the Magyar.

"Oh, the many gypsy maids,
Who have been my lovers true!
They believed that I'd them wed;
That's just what I did not do.

"For my heart it pains me sore,
If but one I chance to see;
Like a slim and slender flower
Is each gentle Romani."

To the following melodies, also taken from the same source, there are no words given.

40 MAGYAR OR HUNGARIAN GYPSY SONGS;

Largo.

These quaint little verses I am permitted by Mr. W. E. Axon, of Manchester, to make use of. They are translations from Wlislocki's "Haideblüten" (1880). The numbers are those given in Wlislocki's book. Some few have already appeared in the *Manchester Quarterly*. The rest are here published for the first time. Mr. Axon is a well-known authority on gypsy lore, and I have to thank him for much kindness during my researches into Romany Songland. I have not been so fortunate with regard to the original version of these songs or their music. It is not always possible to obtain permission to quote from any foreign work, especially from one of the magnitude of the "Haideblüten."

I.

My dear father left this earth
Ere my eyes began to see;
Long ago my mother died,
And my loved one left me.
Few my joys in life would be
But for my fiddle's company.

IV.

A ribbon bright I'll give
For a kiss from my dearest and best,
A mantle warm I'll give
Within her arms to rest;
But should she faithless prove,
A rod I'll buy for my love.

V.

The maiden she wishes for ribbon and rose;
The boy he wishes for bright-chequered hose:
The wife she wishes a baby fine,
But the husband—he wishes for lots of swine!

VIII.

Lord, who has made this earth so fine,
With flowers decked its floor so wide;
Warmed it with the bright sun-rays,
And ordained this Eastern tide;
Lodge with me, now, I pray;
Clean swept my hut to-day,
Clean is the cloth I lay.

IX.

Gaily sing the birds,
The children gaily leap;
We forget the winter's pain
When Whitsuntide we keep.

XIX.

Lonely sits the bird above,
And I am sad, and pine.
Come, my love, and kiss me now,
And ease all pain of mine.

XXII.

When that I was bold and young,
On my arms the fair girls hung;
Now that I am frail and old,
Maidens leave me in the cold.

XXIII.

I a gypsy child was born,
Of a mother all forlorn;
In the long grass I was lain,
None baptized me but the rain.

XXIV.

Oh, thou, my fiddle, art my life!
'Tis thou art my food and my drink;
And when I shall cease to love thee,
My life will be lost, I think.

XXV.

When my heart
Feels sorrow's smart;
When no gold
My purse doth hold,
On my fiddle I play deep,
Until care and hunger sleep.

XXVI.

In autumn the peasant rejoices,
The hunter keeps watch with his gun,
But the gypsy laments and is woeful,
That the sunshine of summer is done.

XXVI.

Though I lived a century, then
Still should I love but young men;
I would not marry one that's old
Though the man were made of gold.

XXXII.

My dear young boy, so fine,
The flowers in thy hat are gay;
But in spite of pretty flowers,
Thy wits are flown away.

44 *MAGYAR OR HUNGARIAN GYPSY SONGS;*

The few lines of music I give next form the chief theme of a gypsy dance, as heard in Vienna.

London society has of late become familiar with many of these wild dance tunes through the medium of the popular Blue Hungarian Band, without which no *réunion* or *fête* has been deemed successful. Through the buzz and hum of many voices above the softly-whispered flirtations of Mayfair maidens and Belgravian bachelors, athwart the grave discussions of thoughtful statesmen, have these wondrous weird melodies stolen, sometimes so soft, and sweet, and low that only Carlyle's simile expresses them—

"Little dewdrops of celestial melody;"

at others, mild, throbbing, and thundering like the angry billows flinging shells on a frightened shore. Always beautiful, always bewitching, what wonder that we have welcomed these interpreters of a world of harmony widely different to our own set, stereotyped ideas of music, and fallen worshippers at the shrine of the Magyar magicians.

" Amid the golden gifts which Heaven
    Has left like portions of its light on earth,
None hath such influence as music hath."

SONGS OF THE GITANOS OR SPANISH GYPSIES.

"The Devil hath not in all his quiver's choice
An arrow for the heart like a sweet voice."
—BYRON.

AMOR Y LIBERTAD.

" Dos cosas en el mundo nie son caras :
Amor y Libertad sólo guerria.
Mi vida diera cel amor en aras
Peso á Libertad mi amor daria."

LOVE AND LIBERTY.

" I sigh for Liberty and Love,
And these suffice for me,
My life I offer up to Love,
My love to Liberty."
—HERACLIO M. DE LA GUARDIA.

SPANISH GYPSY SONGS.

In Spain the Gitanos, or gypsies, are known as *Pharaoh's People*, and there is a strange legend which accounts for their having gained this *sobriquet* current both in Hungary and amongst the Spaniards. "Pharaoh, having conquered all the countries of the known globe with his numerous armies, determined to send a challenge to the Lord God Almighty; God refused to accept the challenge, and, instead, opened a hole in the side of a mountain, and raised a mighty wind; with this wind he drove Pharaoh and his armies into the hole; and the mountain closed on them." On the night of the Feast of St. John there is said to be a sound of voices singing and yelling heard inside the mountain. Pharaoh and his mighty hosts being all shut up, the kings and nations left on the earth rose up in rebellion against the Egyptians, and drove them out of their own land to become wanderers over the rest of the world: hence the gypsies, or wanderers (Zigeuner), that are to be found in every country."

I puzzled for some time over this extraordinary

legend, wondering where I had read or heard something similar to it, but it was not till I had the pleasure of hearing Browning's poem of "The Pied Piper of Hamelin" rendered by Mr. Thomas Brandram in his forcible manner, that it occurred to me where the counterpart of this gypsy fancy was to be found.

> "In Transylvania there's a tribe
> Of alien people, that ascribe
> The outlandish ways and dress
> On which their neighbours lay such stress
> To their fathers and mothers having risen
> Out of some subterranean prison,
> Into which they were trepanned
> Long ago in a mighty band."

The gypsies of Italy and Spain have forgotten their own language, and have formed for themselves a facetious one, called "Gerizonza," or "Ziriguenza," composed of some words of their own invention, and of some Italian and Spanish words, of which they have altered the meaning and inverted the syllables that it might be intelligible only to themselves. The Spanish gypsies are rich in quaint proverbs and terse sayings, many of which are lost to the rest of the world, owing to the strangely untranslatable jargon in which they are clothed. Some of the customs in vogue amongst them have been noted by Mr. Borrow, whose widely-known works on the Spanish gypsies are doubtless familiar to all who are interested in Romany history. For instance, a Gitano will never sell a dead relative's things; he may pawn them, but only if driven to do so as a last resource, and he will redeem them as soon as he can possibly manage to do so; and the horse and donkey of the deceased become as sacred animals to the rest of the tribe. I believe it is a well-known fact that the gypsies of this country will only bury their dead under water, a fact that may be accounted for by the cruel treatment they were for many years subjected to by the Spaniards. They have a saying which shows in what contempt they are held by them. "For that which is unclean by nature thou canst entertain no hope: no washing will turn the gypsy white."—*Ferdousi.*

"All Andalusians, and indeed all Spaniards, have long since made up their minds as to the moral worth of the nomads whom some English writers have found to be so picturesque and interesting; and modern Spain does not differ materially from the dictum laid down by Cervantes, that "gypsies are but a good-for-nothing people, and only born to pick and steal."

I quote these remarks from an admirable article which appeared lately in *The Daily Telegraph*,* on the subject of the trial of Dr. Middleton at Cordova for the murder of the Spanish gypsy in the belfry of the Mezquita, as the Cordovanese still call the beautiful cathedral which was built as a mosque during the domination of the Moors in Southern Spain. This "Romani Chal" was a man of great bodily strength, and of such a ferocious disposition that he was an object of terror to the whole town; nevertheless, the desperado had many sympathizers among the members of his own race, and the trial was attended by hundreds of Gitanos who flocked into the town to see the *estranjero* who had killed their comrade.

To his agreeable summary of the Gitano character the illustrious author of "Don Quixote" might have added that the gypsies have always been the biggest liars on the face of the earth. They are not even to be depended upon in their statements as to the region whence they came, and why they left their country,—although it was doubtless for that country's good. In Spain Zaragoza was formerly the headquarters of the Gitanos, and the residence of the so-called King of the Gypsies; but they are not nearly so numerous at present as was at one time the case in the Castilles, in Arragon, and in La Mancha. Andalusia is now the

* April 10th, 1888.

happiest hunting-ground of the Spanish gypsies, and they gather in greatest numbers at Cordova, in the suburb of Seville, known as La Triana; at Grenada, and Valencia, and at Puerta del Terra of Cadiz. The Andalusian Gitanos are admittedly picturesque, and their pictorial aspect has been admirably rendered in the canvases of John Phillip, of Ansdell, and of Burgess, and in the drawings of Gustave Doré. Nor can it be denied that the young gypsy lassies of the Triana, at Seville, dance with infinite grace and agility, and tell fortunes in the most seductive manner. Ethnologists, again, have always been puzzled to discover the reason for the strong similarity in physiognomy, in manners, and in attainments which exists between the gypsies of the suburb of Seville and those of the environs of Moscow. Their dances are almost identical; there is scarcely any difference between the choregraphic figures indulged in by the Muscovite gypsies and the "seguidillas" and "jotas" in which the Gitanas of the Triana are such adepts; while the distinguished critic, M. Louis Viardot, has drawn attention to the close resemblance of the slow and tender melodies of the Russian to those of the Spanish gypsies. In rough and wild countries there is but a very thin line of demarcation between the gypsy and the brigand, who, on occasion, can be a murderer.

The gypsies are the chosen dancers of the Macarena,

the ragged quarter of Seville, whence Murillo drew his dusty-footed, melon-eating beggar-boys. The Bolero, the Cadiz cachuca, the Malaga dance which describes the bull-fight; seguidillas, manchegas, Malagenas, rondenas, and the famous Romalis, the dance which Tiberius may have seen, and which no one but a gipsy dances in Spain. It is danced to the ancient Oriental music of hand-clapping, and to an old religious Eastern tune, low and melancholy, diatonic, not chromatic, and full of sudden pauses which are strange and startling. It is sung in unison, and has a chorus in which every one joins. Ford, the great authority in Spain, says these tunes are relics of the old Greek and Phœnician music. Even the guitar used by the gypsies of calabash shape is Moorish; it is worn and played just as it was 4,000 years ago, before King Wilkinson came to Egypt and imported the Pharaohs. All these songs are accompanied with castanets, like the rattle of so much summer hail. Very suggestive and stimulating is the sound of castanets to the Spanish ear,— it is as a trumpet to a soldier, or a gun-fire to a sailor. All round the room where these Romany dances are performed, may be heard the dry click-click of these instruments. The gypsies drone a sort of sleepy chant, unceasingly clapping their hands, and the guitar tinkles and chimes as it slowly threads the mazy pattern of the dance.

Truth to tell, the dancing girl is not romantic; no antelope eyes; no black torrents of overflowing hair; no sweeping fringe of eyelash; no serpentine waist; no fairy feet; no moonlight voice. No. She is rather like a sailor's wife at Wapping. She has ropy black hair drawn back behind her ears, in which dangle heavy gold earrings. She wears a large red cauliflowered-pattern gown, and her small neat feet are protected by strong high-lows; she is stout and thick-set, and by no means a sylph. The harebell could never lift its head again if her strong foot once came down upon it. Gradually, as you get accustomed to the dance, you learn to distinguish the dull thump of the heel from the lively quick one-two tap of the toe of her shoes, as, like a young witch of Endor, she seems to swim and float along the room. Every now and then the girl lowers her arms and begins to beat the palms of her brown hands together to some low incantation tune that stirs you strangely by its supernatural and untiring ceaselessness. As for the recitative song, it is more fit for Irish wake-singers or Arab serpent-charmers than for festive dancers, who dance to the pulsation of their own heart-music, and what other extraneous help heaven may send them. The perpetual hand-clapping is exciting, just as the perpetual low beat of the Sioux calabash-drum is exciting. It keeps the mind in a state of fevered tension, highly stimulating to the imagination. The witch dance grows fiercer and faster, the lady of Endor wriggles from side to side, backing and sidling like a shy horse, and the double shuffle going on all the time in a way that no sailor could equal; finally the gypsy girl twists up her pocket handkerchief and flings it into the lap of the most eligible gentleman present. This piece of coquetry is rewarded, or supposed to be rewarded, by a small *douceur* rolled up in the handkerchief and returned with a courteous and gallant bow to the lady.

Longfellow gives a very forcible illustration of the national hatred felt in Spain for the Romany clan, in the second scene of his " Spanish Student," where, in the public square of the village of Guadarrama, the Ave Maria still tolling, a crowd of villagers with their hats in their hands as if in prayer, a group of gypsies in the foreground, and the old Padre Cura standing at the door of his cottage, enter Pancho and Pedro Crespo to read an act of banishment against the gypsies.

PANCHO. Make room, ye vagabonds and gypsy thieves ! Make room for the Alcade and for me !

PADRE C. Keep silence all ! I have an edict here

From our most gracious lord, the King of Spain,
Jerusalem, and the Canary Islands,
Which I shall publish in the market-place.
Open your ears, and listen !
                    Padre Cura
Good day, and pray you hear this edict read.

PADRE C. Good day, and God be with you.
Pray what is it?

PEDRO C. An Act of Banishment against the gypsies.

PANCHO. Silence !

PEDRO C. (*reads*). I hereby order and command
That the Egyptian and the Chaldean strangers,
Known by the name of gypsies, shall henceforth
Be banished from the realm, as vagabonds
And beggars ; and if, after seventy days,
Any be found within our kingdom's bounds
They shall receive a hundred lashes each ;
The second time shall have their ears cut off ;
The third, be slaves for life to him who takes them,
    or burnt as heretics. Signed, I, the King.
Vile miscreants and creatures unbaptized,
You hear the law ! Obey and disappear !

PANCHO. And if in seventy days you are not gone,
Dead or alive I make you all my slaves.

[*The gypsies go out in confusion, showing signs of fear and discontent, Pancho follows*].

Of all gypsy women the Spanish are the most renowned fortune-tellers, " baji," they call it.

" By hedgerows green they strew the leafy bed,
Adroit the lines of palmistry to trace,
Or read the damsel's wishes in her face."

We have many proverbs in use in our country that we do not know the source of. Many of them originate with the quick-witted, black-eyed people of the tents, and of these most are translations from the Spanish Romany; for instance, the homely one, " Where you think there are flitches of bacon there are not even hooks to hang them on," is a gypsy idea; and also, " Steal the pig, and give away the pettitoes for God's sake,"—" Hurtar el puerco, y dar los pies por Dios," and our, " Two heads are better than one," is probably the Gitano's favourite maxim, " Mas veen quatro ojos que dos,"—" Four eyes are better than two."

Notwithstanding the traditional gravity of the Spanish character, it has a vein of humour running through it. The same race which produced the mad seriousness of Don Quixote produced also the comic wisdom of Sancho Panza, with his quaint proverbs and shrewd jests. There was a time when Spanish seemed destined to become the language of the world, and Spain the foremost country, but that time has passed away, and the most the language of the country of olives and wine now offers in the way of superiority is its structure so favourable to poetry, that even those who are not masters of the tongue can find pleasure in reading or listening to the soft musical syllables of Spanish verse and song.

In Longfellow's, gypsy-like drama, "The Spanish Student," there is a genuine gypsy song in the fifth scene, where the gypsies are encamped in the forest, working at a forge.—

Gypsies (at the forge, sing).

" On the top of a mountain I stand,
　With a crown of red gold in my hand,
　Wild Moors come trooping over the lea,
　O how from their fury shall I flee, flee, flee?
　O how from their fury shall I flee?"

"Loud sang the Spanish cavalier,
  And thus his ditty ran :
  God send the gypsy lassie here,
  But not the gypsy man.'

"At midnight, when the moon began
  To show her silver flame,
  There came to him no gypsy man,
  The gypsy lassie came."

[*Original of Gypsy Song at the Forge.*]

"En los sastos de vesque plai me diquélo,
  Doscusañas de sonacai terélo
  Corojai diquélo abillar
  Y-ne asislo chapescar, chapescar."

  "El eray guillabela
   El eray obusno
   Q'abillele Romanala.
   No abillele Caloro."

  "La chimutra se ardela
   A pas-erachi
   El Calo no abillela
   Abillela la romi."

Borrow, in his account of the Zincali, or Gitanos, of Spain, gives this song in the original Romany, as one used in the days of Ferdinand and Isabella, by the gypsy fortune-tellers.

In Spain, one who has been fascinated by the gypsies is called one of the "aficion," or "affection," or "fancy"; he is an "aficianado," or affected unto them, and the people know perfectly what it means, for every Spaniard is at heart a Bohemian.

"He feels what a charm there is in a wandering life, in camping in lonely places, under old chestnut trees, near towering cliffs, 'al pasar del aroyo,' by the rivulets among the rocks." He thinks of the wine-skin and wheaten cakes, when one is hungry on the road, of the mules and tinkling bells, and of the muleteer's song :—

"If thou art sleeping, maiden,
    Awake, and open thy door;
'Tis the break of day, and we must away
    O'er meadow and mount and moor."

"Wait not to find thy slippers,
    But come with thy naked feet;
We shall have to pass through the dewy grass
    And waters wide and fleet."—

of the fire by night, and the "cigarito" smoked till he falls asleep. "Then he remembers the gypsies who came to the camp, and the black-eyed girl who told him his fortune, and all that followed in the rosy dawn, and ever onward into starry night." *

" Y se alegre el alma llena
De la luz de esos luceros."

" And his heart is filled with rapture,
At the light of those lights above."

The following Spanish gypsy songs are taken from Borrow's book, " The Zincali " :—

" My mule so bonny I bestrode,
To Portugal I'd flee ;
And as I o'er the water rode,
A man came suddenly,
And he his love and kindness showed
By setting his dog on me."

Original.
" Me costuné la chori,
Para chalár á Laloró ;
Al nacar de la pani,
Abillo obusno,
Y el chuqual á largo me chibó."

Leland, "The Gypsies."

"Come to the window, sweet love, do,
 And I will whisper there
In Romany a word or two,
 And thee far off will bear."

Original.

"Abillelate á la dicani
 Que io voy te penelár
Una buchi en Calo
 Y despues te liguerár."

"A Gypsy stripling's sparkling eye
 Has pierced my bosom's core,
A feat no eye beneath the sky
 Could e'er effect before."

Original.

"Unas acais callardias,
 Me han vencido,
Como aromali no me vencen otras,
 De cayque nacido."

In Andalusia, where the Moorish influence has left the deepest traces, songs are often to be heard which seem almost a blending of the graceful and yet somewhat sententious quality of the Spanish folk-song and the fierce and passionate melancholy of the gypsy song. Still, though this fusion of two styles renders discrimination difficult as to the sources of each, so much of the wild mystery of the Romany obtains that it is impossible to believe them other than this in origin. All the original gypsy rhymes are in a jargon of Spanish Romany, unintelligible to most Spaniards; but in spite of the hatred and contempt evinced for the down-trodden Gitano, their songs and dances have always found many admirers in the country. Miss Alma Strettell, in a dainty volume of "Spanish and Italian Folk-Songs," devotes several pages to these Gitano or "Flamenco" songs, and gives several specimens of them. She says: "The Flamenco song proper, with its strange, plaintive air, and often elaborate guitar accompaniment, is intended to be sung less by the people than by the 'professional' singers,—either a gypsy or some one taught by them. These singers collect large audiences at the country fairs, or in the little taverns in the gypsy quarter of the towns. Some of them have made a great name in Spain by their improvisations and their expressive singing of these strange lyrics. Many of the Flamenco songs, like the Spanish popular ones, are "bailable" (danceable),—that is, their music is that to which the national dances are performed,—and hence to the charm of the Flamenco song is added the charm of the weird and graceful Flamenco dance; for the dancing of the gypsy women especially has ever been famous in Spain. Very few of these songs are humorous or merry, and those that are are the poorest of their kind. Those who knew these songs and performances in earlier days say that they are becoming corrupted, losing their original and peculiar character, and adopting too much of the more ordinary Spanish tone and style,—becoming "gachonales," as they express it (the word *gachó* being the gypsies' name for the Spaniards). This is attributed to the fact of their having attracted so much attention, and having been introduced into *cafés* where audiences of all classes congregate to hear them. There is, therefore, all the more reason for collecting the most genuine of them, and preserving them from total oblivion.

The most distinctly Flamenco song is the "Seguidilla Gitano, or Jitano," which, unlike its Spanish namesake, consists of four lines only, the first two and the last of which are short, while the third is long; the second and fourth lines rhyme. A prolonged guitar solo ushers in the song, which commences with a long "Ay" wailed out on a succession of 'fioriture." After this the voice pauses; the guitar, again, plays several bars; and then the seguidilla is sung,—the second or third line, whichever is most tragic, or important to the verse, being taken first, and the song closing with the line upon which it began.

Flamenco seguidillas occasionally have the same form as the Spanish ones, but they are then called "Serranas." Diminutives occur at every turn, in the most tragic as well as the most tender passages; the very verbs are conjugated in the diminutive. The impossibility of rendering this strange and charming freak of language into English is one of the many drawbacks which make of a translation but a pale reflection of the original.

The following are "Soleares," which I have been courteously allowed to quote from Miss Strettell's volume :—

"Passing thy door, I said
    An ' Ave Maria ' for thee,
Even as wert thou dead."

" Thy love is like the winds that range,
    And mine is like the unshaken rock,
That knows no change."

" Gypsy maid, when thou art dead,
    Let them with my very heart's blood
Mark the gravestone at thy head."

" I will die, that I may see
    Whether death can end this frenzy,
This thirst for thee."

"I am greater than God in heaven,
Since God will forgive thee never
All that I have now forgiven."

"If I may not take revenge in life,
In death shall my vengeance be,
For I will seek through all the graves
Until I find out thee."

The following are " seguidillas " :—

"Go now, and tell the moon
She need not rise to night,
Or shine, because I have my *comrade's (or lover's) eyes,
To give me light."

The revengeful little song I give next is also a " seguidilla."

" Go to, then!
And Heaven grant thou be
Slain first thyself with that same knife, O comrade,
That thou dost mean for me."

* The use of the word "compañero," or "compañera," is frequent, and it is taken to mean friend, lover, husband, or wife, as the case may be; the English word companion, or comrade, is an insufficient rendering of it, but the only available one.

"Petenera."

"There's that in thee, thou gypsy wife
    Was never seen among thy race ;
Of all thy sorrows, not a sign
    Has passed into thy face."
"No sign has passed into my face,
    Yet sorrow leaves my heart no rest ;
I do not tell my griefs abroad,
    To be the people's jest."

SEGUIDILLA GITANO.

SPANISH PETENERA.

The Gitanos have many varieties of song, some peculiar to the gypsies of one place, such as the "Malagueñas" to Malaga, the "Sevillianas" to Seville;

then Granada has its "Polos" and "Soledads," and the " Fandango con Ritornello" is common to all Spanish gypsy songsters. I have thought it best to give at least one specimen of each, and a word of general apology for their appended translations. It is almost impossible to render at all accurately, and at the same time rhythmically, these quaint gems of Spanish Romany poesy; the words are as out-of-place in our matter-of-fact English language as the music is inappropriate to our pianos; we need the soft starry atmosphere of a Southern night, the rich foliage and glowing colours of the gardens in the city of the Moors, and the dark-eyed gypsy maidens, with their well-used guitars to give the real essence to the "Polo Gitano," or the "Soledad" of Granada; then senseless verses become as enthralling as the grandest epic, the simplest of chords and trills as the music of the spheres; and we are content to know that the world beyond is rolling on in its turbulent, ever-changing course, so long as we may rest under the shade of the gorgeous Alhambra, with only the pomegranate branches between our languid eyes and the dark star-spangled sky, and a band of vivacious Gitanos discoursing sweet music to our willing ears.

" Such sweet compulsion doth in Music lie."

The following is a specimen of the "Soledad" of the gypsies of Granada. These songs are of the same style as the "Complaintes" of the French peasantry.

Second verse.

"Aunque en una cruz te pongas
Vestido de nazareno
Y pegues las tres caidas,
En tu palabra no creo."

The two "Fandangos" which I give next are both favourites with the Gitanos. They are quaint little conceits of Romany gallantry. The first is a "Fandango con Ritornello."

Translation of the "Fandango" words.

"Will you these pearly tears
Leave with me, sweet maiden,
That I may carry them to Granada,
And have them set in gold."

OR SPANISH GYPSIES. 73

The second is also known as a "Fandango."

" How sadly wanders the moon
When clouds are veiling the stars :
So do I grieve my heart
When thou, O love, art away from me."

Peculiar to the Romanies of Malaga is this " Malagueña." I have heard it asserted that the gypsies in this district are of a peculiarly sad temperament. Certainly the tenour of the words of the following is not lively.

Translation of the " Malagueña."

" When the poor mother sees
Her son forsaken and in pain,
In the bitterness of her grief,
On the street fall her tears like rain."

SEGUIDILLAS MANCHEGAS.

This little song is in praise of the Manzanares. It would be something to this effect, if sung in English.

"If I had the choice of two thousand spots,
I still should choose to be near the Manzanares;
To me it is without a rival,
Manzanares, O Manzanares!

"The Manzanares, love, and thine eyes shining,
Beloved maiden, beloved maiden!
The Manzanares, love, and thine eyes shining,
Beloved maiden, beloved maiden!

"Manzanares! Manzanares! let me ever sing of thee;
Sweetest songs of thy wit and spirit,
Let me ever sing of thee."

One thing I cannot understand in this song, and that is the seeming adoration of the river. I thought all gypsies had an instinctive hatred of water, and Spanish gypsies in particular.

The words of the "Polo" which follow are a true specimen of Romany gallantry.

Words of "Polo."

"When you doubt, oh, my beloved!
When you doubt, oh, my beloved!
If I am true to thee,
If I am true to thee,
Devoted, Ah!—
See what I offer thee, Ah!
See what I offer thee
With my whole heart,
My life, my love!"

POLO GITANO Ó FLEMENCO.

OR SPANISH GYPSIES.

LA MALAGUEÑA TIRANA.

LA MALAGUEÑA TIRANA.

There is such a charming German version of this song that I give it here as a translation of "The Malagueña."

" Sing Liebchen weg mir den Kümmer
Singe mir, dŭ süsses Leben, bis mich
Der Ton deines Liedes wieget
In sorglosen Schlŭmmer.

" Denn beiden Klang der Guitarre,
Holder schatz mein, holder schatz mein,
Entfliehen die Schmerzen bei Liedes süssen Zaŭber,
Gequältem Herzen, ja gequältem Herzen enfelt,
Gequältem Herzen, ja gequältem Herzen enfelt.

" Malaga, leb' wohl du Schöne,
Malaga, leb' wohl du Schöne,
Glücklick in dir floss mein Leben ;
Mŭss ich denn, ach, von dir scheiden
Wird doch mein geist dich ŭm,
Schweben, wird doch mein geist dich ŭm.
Lieb ! halt ein ! von dir geshieden find ich im,
Tode nŭr Frieden, Tode nŭr Frieden ; Ach !"

Another "Polo" goes somehow thus:—

"Pretty maiden, deep in my heart
There lies a world of painful love for thee;
Awake from thy slumbers,
Come and soothe my pain.
All my songs of joy have vanished,
Thy presence only gives me rest;
Deprived of the light of thine eyes
What a gloomy melancholy oppresses me.
Ah! what sorrow! Oh! what pain!
Ah! Ah! Ah! Ah!
I die! Ah! I die!"

POLO.

Improvisation seems innate amongst the gypsies as amongst the rest of the population of Spain: love, and hate, and even the commonest things they wish to express are turned into rhyme with extraordinary facility. The language renders this a matter of small difficulty. The lullabies of Malaga have long been celebrated for their extreme beauty, and many of them are in frequent use amongst the gypsies. One may hear a little Romany treasure being lulled, or, more properly speaking, cooed to sleep—since the Spanish word "arrullo" means both the cooing of doves and the lulling of children—by the following:—

> "A dormir va la rosa
> De los rosales;
> A dormir va mi nina
> Porque ya estarde."

A very charming lullaby is quoted by Count Gubernalis in his "Usi Natalizj," which refers to "the Moor" as a very benignant sort of bogey. Strange to say, this song is a special favourite with the mothers of the juvenile Gitani.

> "Isabellita, do not pine
> Because the flowers fade away;
> If flowers hasten to decay,
> Weep not, Isabellita mine.

> " Little one, now close thine eyes,
> Hark! the footsteps of the Moor,
> And she asks from door to door,
> Who may be this child who cries?

"When I was as small as thou,
And within my cradle lying,
Angels came about me flying,
And they kissed me on my brow.

"Sleep then, little baby, sleep,
Sleep, nor cry again to-night,
Lest the angels take to flight,
So as not to see thee weep."

Many of these tunes are probably familiar to lovers of music; Pablo de Sarasate, that most perfect master of the violin, has rendered them so by playing them on many a concert platform. The fire, and life, and soul of the true Spanish gypsy thrill through every note of this marvellous interpreter. In far-off lands we may hear them—these songs of freedom, love, hope, sadness, and despair; songs that have lain dormant many a day till we hear them from one of whom a poet of this nineteenth century has written :—

"This is the young Endymion out of Spain,
Who, laurel-crown'd, has come to us again,
To re-intone the songs of other times in far-off climes."

Farewell then, "campland of the romantic Gitano ; play on, love-bewitched guitars ; sing on, soft Southern voices." Where music dwells—

" Lingering, and wandering as loth to die ;
Like thoughts whose very sweetness yieldeth proof
That they were born for immortality."

—*Wordsworth.*

RUSSIAN ROMANY SONGS;

OR,

SONGS OF THE TZIGGANI.

"Adventurous song,
That with no middle flight intends to soar
Above the Aonian mount, while it pursues
Things unattempted yet in prose or rhyme."
—MILTON.

"Music is the only sensual gratification which mankind may indulge in to excess without injury to their moral or religious feelings."—ADDISON.

RUSSIAN ROMANY SONGS.

"THOSE who have been accustomed to consider the gypsy as a wandering outcast, incapable of appreciating the blessings of a settled and civilized life, or, if abandoning his vagabond propensities and becoming stationary, as one who never ascends higher than the condition of a low trafficker, will be surprised to learn that, amongst the gypsies of Moscow, there are not a few who inhabit stately houses, go abroad in elegant equipages, and are behind the higher orders of the Russians neither in appearance nor in mental acquirements. To the female part of the gypsy colony of Moscow is to be attributed the merit of this partial rise from degradation and abjectness, having from time immemorial so successfully cultivated the vocal art that, though in the midst of a nation by whom song is more cherished and cultivated and its principles better understood than by any other of the civilized globe, the gypsy choirs of Moscow are, by the general voice of the Russian public, admitted to be unrivalled in that most amiable of all accomplishments. It is a fact notorious in Russia that the celebrated Catalani was so enchanted with the voice of one of these gypsy songsters (who, after the former had displayed her whole Italian talent before a splendid audience, stepped forward, and with an astonishing burst of almost angelic melody so enraptured every ear that even applause forgot its duty), that she tore from her own shoulders a shawl of Cashmere which had been presented to her by the Father of Rome, and, embracing the gypsy, insisted on her acceptance of the splendid gift, saying that it had been intended for the matchless songster, which she now perceived she was not."*

Mr. C. G. Leland referring to the musical capabilities of the Russian gypsies, says, " These artists, with wonderful tact and untaught skill, have succeeded in all their songs in combining the mysterious and maddening chorus of the true, wild, Eastern music with that of regular and simple melody intelligible to every Western ear."

A Romany lyric, set by Virginia Gabriel, was more admired in Moscow than in St. Petersburg, which is, perhaps, accounted for by the fact of the gypsies of the former city being always more desirous of learning about the songs of their kindred in other lands.

I am enabled to give the melody of this particular song.

* From "The Zincali," by G. Borrow.

ROMANI.

94 RUSSIAN ROMANY SONGS;

This song, I have been told, is a genuine specimen of gypsy melody. The Wendic songs (except when dance tunes) are generally sung *tremolando*, and very slowly. And there is a peculiarity of all songs indigenous to the Ukraine which is also met with in those of Romany parentage; that is, if a song ends on the dominant or lower octave the last note of the closing verse is sung very softly, and then without a break the new verse begins loud and accented, the only division between the two being such a shake as is described by the German phrase *Bocktriller*.

Russia is so famed for its choral-singing that one turns, with a feeling of expectancy and a certainty that this will be gratified, to the Russian Romanies for some of the wonderful part-songs that are sung by them. Nothing can be more magical than these often extemporized glees, and the Russians know to the full how to appreciate their performance; and pay very highly for the services of the gypsies as musicians.

WENDIC SONG OF GYPSY ORIGIN.

"A large proportion of Russian and other Slavonic songs are of gypsy origin, and are usually in dance rhythm, the dancers marking the time by the stamp of their feet. In short, if we roughly divide the songs of Russia, they will fall into two groups :—(1) songs of a quick, lively *tempo*, commonly sung to dances, in major keys, and in unison ; (2) songs sung very slow, in harmony, and in minor keys. Of the two, the latter are the best and most popular . . . . The later composers of Russia, such as Glinka, Lvoff, Verstovsky, Dargomijsky, Kozlovsky, and others, have been true to the national spirit in their songs. So faithfully have the old national songs been imitated by them that it is hard to distinguish the new from the old productions; and, indeed, some of the modern ones—for instance, Varlamof's "Red Sarafan," and Alabief's "The Nightingale"*—have been accepted as national melodies. Other composers, such as Gurilef and Vassilef Dübüque, have set a number of national airs, especially the so-called gypsy tunes, to modern Russian words in rhyme and four-line stanzas ; and have arranged them with pianoforte accompaniments."

I have quoted the foregoing remarks on Russian song from Sir George Grove's "Dictionary of Music,"

---

* This latter has become more than a national song, for it is in constant and daily use amongst the women who load the boats on the Russian wharves.—L. A. S.

and I have also to acknowledge the source of the little Wendic tune which follows to that same invaluable encyclopædia of harmonic knowledge.

Mr. Charles Wyndham, when in Russia, went with some members of the British Embassy one evening to an encampment, some four miles out of St. Petersburg; he says, "It is quite the fashionable thing to drive out there in the evenings, have supper in a large restaurant near by, and hear the gypsies, in their picturesque costumes, sing, in chorus to the number of about forty, their wild and plaintively melodious native songs."

RUSSIAN GYPSY SONG. (1).

OR, SONGS OF THE TZIGGANI.

Both these melodies are favourites in the Russian Romany camps. They are very harmonious when sung as the gypsies sing them, in chorus. This second one is particularly characteristic of the Muscovite nation, an element of which seems to have found its way into the gypsy tribes settled in Russia.

RUSSIAN GYPSY SONG. (2).

The author of the German Erato, speaking of the Russian national music, says, "It seems in general to bear some resemblance to the ancient airs of Italy, as they existed in their simplest form, long before the refinement of succeeding ages had carried them to their present state of perfection. The Russians, however, had no masters calculated to improve and mature their music; and the composers of their more ancient airs were the untaught children of nature, who accompanied them with such words as flowed spontaneously from their feelings, and that, too, without much regard to the rhyme or regular structure of the stanza ; and this practice still prevails in many parts of the empire.

"These melodies were noted by certain proficients in the musical art, and who, it is naturally supposed, must have been foreigners already settled in the country. More regular stanzas were successively applied by such as had a turn for poetry ; but these bards, if we may judge from the texture of their verses, seem to have been no other than mere rustics or mechanics, whose talents, nature, and passion, not art, had thus called forth.

" The Ukraine has ever been the Provence of the Russian Empire, and, together with the White and the Lesser Russia, still continues to be the nursery of national airs. The inhabitants of those districts may, indeed, be considered as the genuine Troubadours of the nation.

" The Russian songs in their native dress may have little more to recommend them than their extreme *naïveté*, which, how interesting so ever it may be to the common people, would ill undergo a transfusion into another language. The local customs and the particular superstitions to which the songs so frequently allude would, besides, contribute to render a literal version still more awkward and unintelligible to such foreign ears as are accustomed to the more fastidious effusions of the Lyric Muse."

I have, therefore, thought it better just to give the music of the Russian gypsy songs which follow, and which are not set to Romany verse, merely Russian.

RUSSIAN GYPSY SONG.

I only wish some dozen gypsy voices could be bound amongst the leaves of this little volume, to add the necessary touches of life and enthusiastic wildness to these songs of the Tziggani.

RUSSIAN GYPSY SONG.

The following translation was made for me by Mr. Vesseloffsky, of the Russian Consulate-General in London. He apologized for the want of sense in it. Certainly it is an extraordinary composition, and one that is difficult to understand.

"THE VILLAGE PEASANTS."

(VIENSHKI).

I.

"The village peasants
They are merely fools,
Good-for-nothing! White hazel-tree, oh, raspberry-bush!
Vyeryeviewshki vyeryeview, viewshki, viewsky vyer-yeviewshki.
Young lady has little morocco shoes.

2.

"They chop off their fingers, they pull out their [teeth
Not to enter military service,
They do not wish to! White hazel-tree, oh, raspberry-bush!
    Vyeryeviewshki, etc.

3.

"John the Horse-radish is accepted as a recruit;
The whole village began to grieve,
They weep! White hazel-tree, oh, raspberry-bush!
    Vyeryeviewshki, etc.

4.

"That's enough weeping and grieving:
Thou wilt serve not alone
With other people! White hazel-tree, oh, raspberry-bush!
    Vyeryeviewshki, etc.

5.

"On a steep mountlet
There is a wretched inn
Unthatched! White hazel-tree, oh, raspberry bush!
    Vyeryeviewshki, etc.

6.

"The Horse-radish is lying on his side
And smoking a pipe of tobacco.
Makhorka! White hazel-tree, oh, raspberry-bush!
　　Vyeryeviewshki, etc.

7.

"And the old woman, a termagant,
Took a dislike to the smell
Of tobacco! White hazel-tree, oh, raspberry-bush!
　　Vyeryeviewshki, etc.

8.

"She wept, she sobbed,
She ran to the Lieutenant
With a request! White hazel-tree, oh, raspberry-bush!
　　Vyeryeviewshki, etc.

9.

"Thou Lieutenant, my dear,
Be judge in our case
Unimportant! White hazel-tree, oh, raspberry-bush!
　　Vyeryeviewshki, etc.

10.

"He gave his decision in the case:
Five hundred cudgels
Hot! White hazel-tree, oh, raspberry-bush!
 Vyeryeviewshki, etc.

11.

"Thou old woman don't be cross,
Make your peace with the lodger,
The Horse-radish! White hazel-tree, oh, raspberry-bush!
 Vyeryeviewshki, etc.

A song which a female gypsy sang to Mr. Borrow, at Moscow, commenced in this way,

"Her head is aching with grief,
As if she had tasted wine,"

and ended thus,

"That she may depart in quest
Of the lord of her bosom,
And share his joys and pleasures."

RUSSIAN GYPSY DANCE.

This last is one of the favourite dance tunes of the gypsies of Moscow. Perhaps in no country in the world do these alien people contribute so much to the amusement of the general populace as in Russia; and an evening spent at one of the camps is amongst the *divertissements* first suggested to a visitor either to St. Petersburg or Moscow. There he will hear the famous gypsy songs, and see the famous gypsy dancing, and he will find sufficient entertainment in these even to

> " Last out a night in Russia,
> When nights are longest there."

ANGLO-ROMANY SONGS.

"Gypsy music is a weed of the strangest form, colour, and leafage—one hardly to be planted in any orderly garden."—CHORLEY.

" 'Twill ever be the same old song
Of gypsy tinkers all day long;
And he who cannot sing it more,
May sing it over, as before."

ANGLO-ROMANY SONGS.

Bluff Prince Hal set himself an almost impossible task when he thought " to drink with every tinker in his own language." There is a very evident cosmopolitanism amongst all gypsies, but it does not extend to the stranger in the camp; and there is nothing more difficult than for the Gorgio to enter the portals of the Romany world if he be not possessed of that nameless something which proclaims him one with that strange band who were neither the " Fatherhood of God," nor the " Brotherhood of man."

A man must be *tatchey Romany* (real Romany) before he can properly drink with the tinker in his own language. We have all of us probably some recollections of encounters with the wandering tribes we call gypsies; many of us may, perhaps, have only some dim and indistinct memories, not untinged with fear, of the panniered ladies and black-eyed gentlemen whom, with their tawny families, we came upon suddenly in some woodland scene—strange, Murillo-like groups in the midst of homely English landscape. Some few of us may have sufficiently overcome our nervousness and disinclination as to make some friendly advances upon such occasions, and have, perhaps, in consequence, preserved a more kindly regard for them, though this regard is so hedged about with the prickly thorns of long-standing prejudice and rooted dislike, that it can scarcely be said to lead us to adopt any plan that should have for its object the amelioration of the Romany people. And yet there is much that is worthy of study, and more that commands admiration in the gypsy character; and the honour that is always said to exist among thieves is also to be found amongst them. They have, it is true, many strange, and indeed repulsive, customs, which cannot but render them aliens to us. Their character may best be learnt from their proverbs, of which they have an inexhaustive store, although many of them are utterly untranslatable, save to the initiated in what is known as the Romany tongue, or Thieves' Latin. The gypsies have many names in the different countries of the globe, and some of the ideas which originated these titles are worth studying. For instance, the Dutch, apprehending that they came from Egypt, called them "Heydenen" (heathens); the Moors and Arabians know them as "Charanu," or robbers; in Hungary and in Spain they are "Pharaoh's People" (the legend which gave this extraordinary name I have referred to elsewhere); in Germany they are known as "Zigeuner," or wanderers; the common people of the Fatherland used to call the land-tramps which overran their country, "Zihegan," before the gypsies were ever heard of. In Transylvania, Waldachia, and Moldavia they are "Cyganis," and in Turkey and other eastern countries, "Tschingenes." With us they are known as tinkers, horners, muggers, or potters; and Kirk Yetholm, one of the best-known of the border gypseries, boasts now of a Tinkler's Row. The gypsies' thieving propensities are so proverbial, that one would as soon look for the mullet in the hen-coop as an honest gypsy, though even in this they have a code of honour which prevents them helping themselves to anything that is to be found within a certain distance of their camp. One of their proverbs is, that "What God kills is better than what man kills," though I am afraid they rarely adhere to the truth of it; and it is much more the devil's work than either God's or man's that brings fish, flesh, and fowl to the Romany stew-pot.

In many places the gypsies support themselves by rope-dancing and tricks of legerdemain; while the women find occupation in fortune-telling, the interpretation of dreams, and the like. They have a certain degree of natural talent for music, and are often respectable performers on the violin, flute, Jews-harp, etc.

The following is a specimen of an old English gypsy dance :—

GYPSY DANCE.

Lord Lytton, in his novel "The Disowned," gives a type of gypsy song that is certainly worthy of insertion amongst a collection of Romany lyrics. The chorus of it, he says, was chanted in full diapason by the whole group of gypsies, with the additional force of emphasis that knives, feet, and fists could bestow.

THE GYPSY'S SONG.

" The king to his hall, and the steed to his stall,
   And the cit to his bilking board ;
But we are not bound to an acre of ground,
   For our home is the houseless sward.

" We sow not, nor toil, yet we glean from the soil
   As much as its reapers do ;
And wherever we rove, we feed on the cove,
   Who gibes at the mumping crew.
      Chorus.—So the king to his hall, etc.

" We care not a straw for the limbs of the law,
   Nor a fig for the *cuffin queer ;* *
While Hodge and his neighbour shall lavish and labour
   Our tent is as sure of its cheer.
      Chorus.—So the king to his hall, etc."

" The worst have an awe of the *harman's* † claw,
   And the best will avoid the *trap ;* ‡
But our wealth is as free of the bailiff's *see*,
   As our necks of the twisting *crap*. §
      Chorus.—So the king to his hall, etc.

* Magistrates.   † Constable.   ‡ Bailiff.   § Gallows.

"They say it is sweet to win the meat
For the which one has sorely wrought ;
But I never could find that we lacked the mind,
For the food that has cost us nought.

    Chorus.—So the king to his hall, etc.

"And when we have ceased from our fearless feast,
Why, our *jigger** will need no bars ;
Our sentry shall be on the owlet's tree,
And our lamps the glorious stars.

    Chorus.—So the king to his hall, etc.

The following charming little Romany Lullaby I quote from George Borrow's " Romano Lavo Lil."

"Sleep thee, little tawny boy !
  Thy mother's gone abroad to spae,
Her kindly milk thou shalt enjoy,
  When home she comes at close of day.

"Sleep thee, little tawny guest !
  Thy mother is my daughter fine :
As thou dost love her kindly breast,
  She once did love this breast of mine."

* Door.

ROMANY VERSION.

"Jaw to sutlers, my tiny chal,
    Your die to dukker has jall'd abri,
At rarde she will wel palal,
    And tute of her tud shall pie.

"Jaw to lutherum, tiny baw!
    I'm teerie deya's purie mam,
As tute cams her tud canaw
    Thy deya meerie tud did cam."

The wrinkled old beldame, who never fails to form part of the household of a gypsy camp, may sometimes be heard crooning this little ditty as she rocks the Romany cradle beneath the leafy shade of some forest monarch.

Another song from the same source is an Anglo-Romany love-song.

"I'd choose as pillows for my head
    Those snow-white breasts of thine;
I'd use as lamps to light my bed
    Those eyes of silver shine.
O lovely maid, disdain me not,
    Nor leave me in my pain;
Perhaps 'twill never be my lot
    To see thy face again."

(ORIGINAL) "CAMO GILLIE."

"Pawnie birks
My men-engri shall be
Yackors my dudes
Like ruppeny shine.
Atch, meerry chi!
Ma jal away:
Perhaps I may not dick tute
Kek romi."

It may not be generally known that the popular English nursery rhyme, "Little Bingo," is of gypsy parentage.

"LITTLE BINGO."

"A farmer's dog leap'd over the stile,
His name was little Bingo.
There was B with an I, I with an N.
N with a G, G with an O—
There was B I N G O,
And his name was little Bingo.

"The farmer lov'd a cup of good ale,
And called it very good stingo.
There was S with a T, T with an I, I with an N,
N with a G, G with an O,
There was S T I N G O,
And called it very good stingo."

ANGLO-ROMANY SONGS.

"The farmer lov'd a pretty young lass,
And gave her a wedding-ring, O.
There was R with an I, I with an N,
N with a G, G with an O,
There was R I N G O,
And gave her a wedding ring, O.

Now is not this a nice little song?
I think it is, by Jingo!
There was J with an I, I with an N,
N with a G, G with an O,
There was J I N G O.
I think it is, by Jingo!

"LITTLE BINGO."

ENGLISH GYPSY NURSERY RHYME.

From George Borrow's "Romano Lavo Lil" are the two following Anglo-Romany songs. The one known as "The Youthful Earl" ("The Temeskoe Rye") is one of the most charming compliments ever paid to gypsy beauty.

"THE YOUTHFUL EARL."

"Said the youthful earl to the gypsy girl,
    As the moon was casting her silver shine :
' Brown little lady, Egyptian lady,
    Let me kiss those sweet red lips of thine.' "

Romany rendering.

" Penn'd the temeskoe rye to the Romany chi,
    As the moon was dicking prey eende dui :
' Rinkeny tawni, Romany rawni,
    Mook man choom teero, gudeo mui.' "

The second is "My Romany Lass" ("Miro Romany Chi"), and savours somewhat of Salt Lake City.

"MY ROMANY LASS."

" As I to the town was going one day,
My Romany lass I met by the way ;
Said I, ' Young maid, will you share my lot ? '
Said she, 'Another wife you've got.'
' Ah, no,' to my Romany lass I cried ;
' No wife have I in the world so wide ;
And you my wedded wife shall be,
If you will consent to come with me.' "

" MIRO ROMANY CHI."

Romany rendering.

"As I was jawing to the gav yeck divvus,
I met on the drom miro Romany chi ;
I pootch'd lass whether she come sar manda,
And she penn'd tu sar wafo rommadis ;
O mande there is kek wafo romady,
So penn'd I to miro Romany chi ;
And I'll kair tute miro tatcho romadi
If you but pen tu come sar mande."

The Romany maiden's answer is not chronicled.
Perhaps, like the heroine of the old song, " Hunting-

tower," she found her suspicions groundless, and was content to take her gypsy sweetheart at his word, as Jean did the Laird of Blair Athole.

In the so-called Metropolitan gypseries at Wandsworth, Hampstead, Hampton, and in others, the following gypsy whittling song may often be heard:—

"Can you rokra Romany?
Can you play the bosh?
Can you jal adrey the staripen?
Can you chin the cost?"

Translation.
"Can you speak the Romany tongue?
Can you play the fiddle?
Can you eat the prison loaf?
Can you cut and whittle?

This tune will be known to many, especially to Anglo-Indians, as "Money makes the mare to go." Is this one more link in the chain which connects the gypsies with Hindustan?

The drinking-chorus which I give next is *tatchey Romany* (real gypsy) :—

"Here the gypsy gemman see,
With his Romany jib, and his rome and dree,
Rome and dree, rum and dry,
Rally round the Romany Rye."

Which may also be said of the following, known as a "Kettle-mender's song" :—

"The Romany chi
And the Romany chal
Shall jaw tasanlor
To drab the bawlor,
And dook the gry
Of the farming rye"

Translation.

"The Romany churl,
And the Romany girl
To-morrow shall hie
To poison the sty,
And bewitch on the mead
The farmer's steed.

George Borrow, in one of his books, gives a song which he says is known to be the oldest specimen of English gypsy poetry in existence; but as he does not give any translation of it, I have not thought it necessary to quote it.

The gypsies' preference for pork, in any shape or form, is so well known that the song which follows needs no introduction to the reader.

"DEAD PIG."

"I went to the farmhouse,
  Where I knew a pig had died,
And to get it I implored 'em,
  Till I pretty nearly cried.

"But the lady wouldn't give it,
  And she 'inted rather free,
As 'twas poisoned by some gypsy
  And that gypsy man was *me*."

"MŪLLO BĀLOR."

"Oh! I jāssed to the ker,
  An' I tried to māng the bālor,
Tried to māng the mūllo bālor,
  When I jāssed to the ker.

"But the rāni wouldn't del it,
  For she pénnas les os drabbered,
For she pénnas les os drabbered
  Penn's the Rómany chál had drábbed the bālor."

Mr. C. G. Leland, in his admirable collection of Anglo-Romany songs, provides lovers of Romany lore with a very wide field in the poetry and rhymes he has given peculiar to the gypsy tribes. For *naïveté* his little poem which I have quoted from his volume of songs could scarcely be equalled, save, perhaps, in the coquette tongue of the French.

> " Sī mándy sos tīro chavo,
>   Sī tute sos mīri dye,
> Kāméssa del mandy a chūmer?
>   Kekker mī rūzno rye!
>
> " Awer mī shóni kek tīro chávo,
>   Awer tūte shán kek miri dye:
> Adóvás a waver covva;
>   Avo, mī kushto rye!"
>
> " ' If I were your little baby,
>   If you were my mother old,
> You would give me a kiss, my darling.'
>   'Oh, sir, you are far too bold.'
>
> " ' But as you are not my mother,
>   But as I am not your son;
> Ah, that is another matter,
>   So maybe I'll give you one.' "

And for its beauty the love-song which follows from the same source, may safely dispense with any apology for its insertion.

> "Tu chan i chóne adré o hev,
> Mi déari kāmeli rāni ;
> Te wāver fóki shan o báv,
> Kun gávla tūt, fón mán y."

> "The moon soft shining o'er the heaven,
> My darling, seems like thee ;
> And other folk are but the cloud,
> That hide thy face from me."

The following song is known as "Hugh of Lincoln," and is familiar to most London gypsies with its quaint air all runs, and trills, and "grace-notes."

"HUGH OF LINCOLN."

> "Down in merry, merry Scotland
> It rained both hard and small,
> Two little boys went out one day,
> All for to play with a ball.

> "They tossed it up so very, very high,
> They tossed it down so low ;
> They tossed it into the Jew's garden,
> Where the flowers all do blow.

"Out came one of the Jew's daughters,
    Dressed in green all,
  'If you come here, my fair pretty lad,
    You shall have your ball.'

"She showed him an apple as green as grass,
    The next thing was a fig;
  The next thing a chérry as red as blood,
    And that would 'tice him in.

"She set him on a golden chair,
    And gave him sugar sweet,
  Laid him on some golden chest of drawers,
    Stabbed him like a sheep.

"Seven foot Bible
    At my head and my feet,
  If my mother pass by me,
    Pray tell her I'm asleep."

Mr. Groome gives this version of "Hugh of Lincoln" in his "In Gypsy Tents;" but there are several; one is to be found in Miss Charlotte S. Burne's "Shropshire Folk-Lore, Ballads," etc. Speaking of this song, Miss Burne says:—"In the year 1255 the Jews of Lincoln were charged with the crucifixion of a little Christian boy on June 29th. The story forms the theme of Chaucer's 'Prioress' Tale.'"

In Borrow's "Romany Rye" are to be found the following famous gypsy verses, known as "Poisoning the Porker."

> "To mande shoon, ye Romany chals
> Who besh in the pus about the yag,
> I'll pen how we drab the baulo,
> I'll pen how we drab the baulo.

> "We jaws to the drab-engro ker,
> Trin horsworth there of drab we lels,
> And when to the swety back we wels,
> We pens we'll drab the baulo,
> We'll have a drab at a baulo.

> "And then we kairs the drab opré,
> And then we jaws to the farming ker,
> To mang a beti habben,
> A beti poggado habben.

> "A rinkeno baulo there we dick,
> And then we pens in Romano jib;
> Wust lis odoi opré, ye chick,
> And the baulo he will lel lis,
> The baulo he will lel lis.

"Coliko, coliko saulo we
Apopli to the farming ker
Will lel and mang him mullo,
Will wel and mang his truppo.

"And so we kairs, and so we kairs;
The baulo in the rarde mers;
We mang him on the saulo,
And rig to the tan the baulo.

"And then we toves the wendror well
Till sose the wendror in Zion se,
Till kekkeno drab's adrey lis,
Till drab there's kek adrey lis.

"And then his truppo well we hatch,
Kin levinor at the kitchema,
And have a kosko habben,
A kosko Romano habben.

"The boshom engro kils, he kils,
The tawnie juva gils, she gils
A puro Romano gillie,
Now shoon the Romano gillie."

The translation, also given by Mr. Borrow, is as follows :—

"Listen to me, ye Romany lads who are seated in the straw about the fire, and I will tell how we poison the porker, I will tell how we poison the porker.

"We go to the house of the poison-monger,* where we buy three pennies' worth of bane, and when we return to our people we say we will poison the porker, we will try and poison the porker.

"We then make up the poison, and then we take our way to the house of the farmer, as if to beg a bit of victuals, a little broken victuals.

"We see a jolly porker, and then we say in Romany language, ' Fling the bane yonder amongst the dirt, and the porker will soon find it, the porker will soon find it.'

Early on the morrow, we will return to the farm-house, and beg the dead porker, the body of the dead porker.

"And so we do, even so we do; the porker dieth during the night; on the morrow, we beg the porker, and carry to the tent the porker.

"And then we wash the inside well, till all the inside is perfectly clean, till there's no bane within it, not a poison grain within it.

"And then we roast the body well, send for ale to the

* The apothecary.

alehouse, and have a merry banquet, a merry Romany banquet. The fellow with the fiddle plays, he plays; the little lassie sings, she sings an ancient Romany ditty, now hear the Romany ditty.

The gypsies have many strange little verses regarding their belief or hope of some future state of existence; for instance, there is something of poetry and not a little of reason in

"O soro divvúsko divvus
Ko si adúvvel?
Kún tu sovess' aláy
Kéti boro Dúvvel."

"Tell me what is
The Judgment Day?
It is when unto God
You dream away."

Mr. F. H. Groome, speaking of gypsy epitaphs in his fascinating book of sketches, entitled "In Gypsy Tents," gives several specimens; amongst others, this touching little memento of a beloved Romany baby:—

"Farewell, thou little blooming bud,
Just bursting into flower;
We give thee up; but oh, the pain
Of this last parting hour."

And one inscribed on the tombstone of "Lucretia Smith, Queen of the Gypsies," in the churchyard at Beighton, Derbyshire :—

> " Happy soul, thy days are ended,
> All thy mourning days below;
> Go, by angel guards attended,
> To the sight of Jesus go."

They have another saying, which shows that the gypsy has some very keen knowledge of the Gorgio's character :—

> " If foky kek jins bute,
> Mà sal at lende;
> For sore mush jins chomany
> Thate tute kek jins."

> " Whatever ignorance men may show,
> From none disdainful turn;
> For every one doth something know
> Which you have yet to learn."

That the Romanies are essentially a love-making people is evident from the many pretty little scraps of prose and poetry that are scattered over their literature, if one may class as literature the fugitive gems constituting Romany book-lore.

The following lines are so quaint and so full of the tenderness that is often lacking in our insular courtships, that I cannot refrain from quoting them:—

"Si mīri chūmya shan kūshti to hā,
Tu nasti hatch bóckalo, déari ajā."

"If kisses of mine were good to eat,
You shouldn't go hungry long, my sweet."

"The little bubbles floating on the wave
Are all soft kisses which the west wind gave;
The luscious glow upon the peach's face
Bears blushing witness to the sun's embrace.
And those two dimples, sweet, that come and go,
Tell tales of true-love kisses, is't not so?"

In nothing is gypsy family love more visible than in the closeness with which one death in a tent is followed by another; and the fresh flowers beneath the glass shades on most gypsy graves tell a tale of unforgotten grief.

Many curious roadside ceremonies are performed by the gypsies as they wend their way from place to place; for instance, that of laying *patrins*, or heaps of grass or leaves, at cross-roads, to indicate to loiterers the route that they must follow. Both in Germany,

Norway, and in India the *patrin* chase is a familiar institution.

All over England the water-wagtail is known as the *Rómano chiriklo*, or "gypsy magpie," and they believe that its appearance foretells a meeting with other gypsies, kinsfolk, or strangers, according as it flies or does not fly away; and they have a formula which they chant on meeting one.

"Is it any kin to me? it will fly, it will fly;
Is it any kin to me? it will fly, it will fly."

It is also believed that a gypsy lad killing one of these birds is sure to have a lady for his sweetheart (suvéla raúni).

Gypsy riddles, too, are remarkable for their quaint originality. They have one in rhyme, often sung by children, descriptive of a cherry:—

"Riddle me, riddle me, red coat,
A stick in his hand, a stone in his throat,
Riddle me, riddle me, rōti tōt."

And a hedgehog is thus designated. "As I was a-going along the road one day, I met a man coming through the hedge with a lot of pins and needles on his back." "It plays in the wood, and sings in the wood, and gets its master many a penny," expresses very tersely the gypsy's estimate of a fiddle. Mr. Groome has a very great opinion of the gypsies as performers on the latter. The Welsh gypsies he admits are beautiful harp players; but he stands up for the good old English rollicking gypsy fiddler; and he says, in speaking of their singing, " Gatherers of old songs and melodies may go further afield than Little Egypt, to come back emptier-handed than if they had loitered an hour beside the tents. Myself, I know the tune but not the notes, so am just as serviceable as an inkless pen; but let the first musician that lights on Boswell, Stanley, Lovell, or Herne secure some of the lovely airs."

Mr. Groome's experiences among the gypsies are entirely confined to this country. He says, "They profess to be, and are, real experiences. My gypsies are genuine. My gypsy women are not the gypsy women of the theatre; they do not wear short red petticoats, worked at the bottom with black cabalistic signs, still less silk stockings or antique sandals on their feet, or turbans on their heads; nor are they called 'Zarah' or 'Zillah.' My gypsy men never, by any accident, swathe their legs in linen bandages, cross-gartered with red worsted lace; the nearest approach they ever make to a brigand's jacket is a velveteen shooting-coat, much the worse for wear; and altogether their appearance is suggestive of a cross between a debauched gamekeeper and a Staffordshire pot-hawker."

George Borrow, in that most incomprehensible book, "Lavengro, the Scholar, the Gypsy, the Priest," gives very conflicting accounts of the gypsies of his acquaintance. It is a book that can content no one. It hovers between romance and reality, and can have done but little towards establishing a more friendly feeling between Gorgios and Romanies. The character of Lavengro, to use the words of a writer on the subject in *Fraser's Magazine* (March, 1851), "is an impossible medley of Orlando Furioso and Peregrine Pickle."

For the tune of the following song I am indebted to Miss Burne, of Shropshire folk-lore fame; and for the words to Mr. Groome, who quotes them in his " In Gypsy Tents."

COLD BLOWS THE WIND.

ANGLO-ROMANY SONGS.

The following gypsy love-songs were noted down by Miss Burne from a family named Wharton, habitually travelling in Shropshire and Staffordshire.

"My mother sent me for some water,
 Over the stepping-stones high and dry;
My foot slipped, and in I tumbled,
 My true love came whistling by.

"My mother said as I shouldna have him,
 Cos that he would break my heart.
I don't care what my mother tells me,
 I shall take my true love's part.

"He will buy me silks and satins,
 He will buy me a guinea-gold ring,
He will buy me a silver cradle,
 For to lap my baby in."

"My chap's gone a sailor for to be,
 He's gone across the deep blue sea;
When he do return how happy I shall be,
 I'm going to marry a navy!

"I'm going to marry a chap in blue,
 He is a navy, and his eye dark blue,
And O! I know that he loves me true.
 I'm going to marry a navy!"

"I'll have my petticoat bound wi' red,
And the lad I love I'll beg his bread,
And then my parents 'll wish me dead.

"And I'll go down to yanders mill,
And I'll lie down and cry my fill,
And every tear shall turn a mill."

This song of "The Cruel Mother" was also sung by Eliza Wharton and her brothers. It is a variant of a standard ballad in Kinloch's and Motherwell's collections.

"THE CRUEL MOTHER."

"There was a lady, a lady of York,
(*Ri fol i diddle i gee wo!*)
She fell a-courting in her own father's park,
Down by the greenwood side, O!

" She leaned her back against the stile [read thorn]
  (*Ri fol i diddle i gee wo !*)
  There she had two pretty babes born,
  Down by the greenwood side, O !

" And she had nothing to lap 'em in,
  (*Ri fol i diddle i gee wo !*)
  But she had a penknife sharp and keen,
  Down by the greenwood side, O !

" She did not care if they felt the smart,
  (*Ri fol i diddle i gee wo !*)
  There she stabbed them right through the heart,
  Down by the greenwood side, O !

" She wiped the penknife in the sludge,
  (*Ri fol i diddle i gee wo !*)
  The more she wiped it the more the blood showed,
  Down by the greenwood side, O !

" As she was walking in her own father's park,
  (*Ri fol i diddle i gee wo !*)
  She saw two pretty babes playing with a ball,
  Down by the greenwood side, O !

" 'Pretty babes, pretty babes, if you were mine,
  (*Ri fol i diddle i gee wo !*)
  I'd dress you up in silks so fine,'
  Down by the greenwood side, O !

" 'Dear mother, dear mother, when we were thine,
(*Ri fol i diddle i gee wo!*)
You dressed us not in silks so fine,'
Down by the greenwood side, O!
" Here we go to the heavens so high,
(*Ri fol i diddle i gee woo!*)
You'll go to bad when you do die!
Down by the greenwood side, O!"

A truly horrible ditty, and rendered doubly so from the lips of children; Miss Burne's account of these poor little tent mortals is very distressing. The carol which follows is a favourite with gypsy children.

GYPSY CHILDREN'S CHRISTMAS CAROL.

Now Christ-mas day is draw-ing near at hand, Come sarve the Lord, And be at His com-mand. And for a por-tion God He will pro-vide, And give a bles-sing to his soul be-side.

Miss Burne has told me many pitiful stories of the state of these poor little wanderers in the Midland counties, as free as the birds in the air, yet held in the tightest of bondage, the bondage of ignorant vice. The gypsy children appeal to every Gorgio's sympathy; their fathers and mothers have chosen for themselves the lives of vagabonds and outcasts; but the little children, shall they be allowed to choose for themselves, or rather, to follow the only example held up to them? At least let us try what we can to show them the two roads; and then if it be true that the instinct is there, that "no washing can make the gypsy white," and that but one path lies before them— the path to Bohemian sloth and wildness, then we can feel that at any rate the sign-posts, or as the Romanies would say, the *patrines*, were not wanting on the highroad of life.

"The Moon Shines Bright" is a gypsy variant of a well-known old Shropshire carol.

" Christ made a trance one Sunday view,
All with His own dear hands.
He made the sun clear, and the moon
Like the water on dry land.

" All for the saving of our souls,
Christ died upon the cross;
What shall we do for our Saviour,
Like He has done for us?

"O, teach your children well, dear man,
    And teach them while they're young,
For better 'twill be for your soul, dear man,
    When you are dead and gone.

"To-day, dear man, you might be alive,
    Worth many thousand pound,
And to-morrow, dear man, you may be dead,
    And your corpse laid in the ground.

"With a turf all at your head, dear man,
    And another at your feet,
Your good deeds and your bad ones all
    Before the Lord shall meet.

"There are six days in the week, dear man,
    For this poor labouring man,
And the seventh day to serve the Lord,
    Both Father and the Son.

"Hell is deep, and hell is dark,
    And hell is full with faults,
May the Lord give us grace in every place,
    And to pray to our ending day."

"THE MOON SHINES BRIGHT."

Christ made a trance one Sunday view, all with His own dear hands. He made the sun clear, and the moon Like the water on dry land.

Eliza Wharton sang the next carol for Miss Burne.

" Now Christmas Day is drawing near at hand,
Come sarve the Lord, and be at His command,
And for a portion God He will provide,
And give a blessing to his soul beside.

" Go down in yonder garden where flower grows by ranks,
Go down upon your knees, and turn the good Lord thanks ;
Go down upon your knees, and pray both night and day,
And get a blessing for His sake, who washed our sins away.

"And little childerin, they larn to cuss and swear,
Afore they knows one word of their Lord's prayer;
They're patched and painted, dressed in idle stuff,
Likes if God had not made them fine enough."

The tune of the following song is Romany; it is really a perversion of Goethe's "King of Thule," and was noted down by Mr. F. H. Groome, from some of his gypsy fiddler friends.

"There jiv'd a Romano krallis,
And a tátcheno rei was he,
'Fore yoi mulli'd a kurruv o' sónakei,
Del'd lésti his pirini.

"There was chíchi yuv kom'd so mishto
Sorkon chairos he haw'd he would pi
'Vri adúvel, and out o' yuk's yokàs,
The pani nash'd avri.

"And when lésti vel'd to mullain,
Yuv pen'd as how sorkon gav,
Yuv del'd to the krallis arter him,
But kek o' the kurrúv a lav.

"Yuv besh'd by the krallisko hobben
With his kistaméngros sor
'Dré his dadus's bóro kamóra
Odoi by the doriove shore.

"Kek komi the puro piamóngro
The jívobens yog should pi
For he wusser'd the komelo kurrúv
Right alé dré the doriov's zi."

"Yuv dik'd lis pelin, pórderin'
Yal alé dré the pani loon,
Aud his yokas pánder'd their kokoré
And yuv was a gillo coon."

ENGLISH ROMANY SONG.

(Sung to the tune of "Billy Taylor.")

"Dórdi the toóvin' tatto-páni,
Dórdi the tátcheno Romani chals!
With the bóshoméngro kellin'
Muk us giv our gílli, Pals,

    Júkels ful for prastamengros,
    Mas for Kaúlos on the drom;
    Kóngeris was but kair'd for ráshis,
    Stáribens 'cos dinlos kom.

"What's a puknius, so si wóngar,
What's to be a bóro rei?
So as we lels a kúshto jívoben
Why should we kesser sar or kei?

    Júkels ful for prastamengros, etc.

"Adré the divvus pennin hukabens
All about the tem we jas,
And adré the raati in a gránzi
Choomer our raklis opré the kas.

 Júkels ful for prastamengros, etc.

"That's the reís vardo with its kistaméngros
Prásters féreder, who might pen?
Or that the wúdrus of the romer'd rauni
Diks any féreder komoben?

 Júkels ful for prastamengros, etc.

"Jívoben's kair'd ó dósta kóvas,
Méndi 'll kek kesser how they av :
Muk them roker about decorum
Who are atrást for their kúshto nav.

 Júkels ful for prastamengros, etc.

"Then kúshto bokh to tan and sásta
Kúshto bokh to kaúlos sor,
And kúshto bokh to the nóngo chávis :
Muks pen sor on us *Amushaw*,

 Júkels ful for prastamengros," etc.

Some few weeks ago I spent a day amongst the gypsies at Plaistow. Upton Lane and the Plaistow Marshes are very favourite *locaux* for the tents and vans of the Metropolitan gypsies, and quite a colony of Lees and Smiths are to be found there during the winter months. From one of the former I obtained the words of the following song. She was a pretty young woman, with a singularly sweet and pathetic voice. She bade me welcome to her small domicile— a van, which her husband had cut out with a single penknife—with a womanly graciousness which might have been envied by many a hostess. She was occupied in making tea, and otherwise preparing the midday meal, which consisted, besides the beverage before named, of a small piece of mouldy-looking bread, a scrap of cheese, and a parcel of brown sugar. A small boy was cutting some wood over the open stove. This, together with the table, which was also a chest of drawers, the bed, and three wooden stools, constituted the *ameublement* of the movable dwelling. I had considerable difficulty in finding a resting-place for my arm on the narrow ledge which had to serve the double purpose of *écritoire* and family dining-table. The story of this poor woman's life, which piece by piece I gathered during the short time I spent with her, was a sad one. She had left a good situation as housemaid, which, by a careful mother's training, she had been most satisfactorily able to fill, to become the wife of a gypsy good-for-nothing, who seemed to depend almost entirely on her for maintenance—a dependence which necessitated her tramping for hours daily, laden with gilt jewellery, shell ornaments, and pin-cushions, and the other wares that find favour at the area door in the London suburbs.

"THE SQUIRE AND THE GYPSY MAID."

" One spring morning early a squire was straying
    Over the beauteous lands that nature gave birth,*
    The primrose bloomed forth and the young lambs were straying;
    He sighs, ' I am lonely on this beauteous earth.'

" ' But what are those notes that echo the valley?
    Yon smoke that's ascending, it shall be my guide.
    Let her be what she may, *both*† wealthy or lowly,
    I'll swear by the powers I'll make her my bride!'

" He had not strayed far when struck with such beauty,
    He'd scarcely trot‡ far in the deep woody dell,
    By the side of the tent two eyes shone like diamonds,
    And there he beheld the dark gypsy girl.

---

* I think the right version of this line should be " To which nature gave birth." My gypsy vocalist was not particular either as to rhyme or rhythm.

    † " Or wealthy, or lowly."   ‡ " Gone far."

"'Shall I tell you your fortune?' 'Oh, dearest, I
    know it—
The fortune I crave for, is you for my bride;
You shall live in a castle surrounded by servants,
Silks and fine satins shall be your attire;
My sweet gypsy bride shall be looked on with
    envy
As she rides in her carriage the wife of a squire.'

"'You promise to me a grand proposal,
You promise to make me as rich as a queen;
Throw them all to the dirt, while I so light-
    hearted
Can ride on my neddy that stands on the green.'

"'So fly with me now, in a few months we'll marry,
As man and as wife together can dwell.
I am not of age, that's the reason I tarry,
But I am sure for to marry the dark gypsy girl!'

"'O you are a squire, and I'm a poor gypsy:
Both wealth and great beauty are at your command
There's more honour and virtue in the poor and
    the lowly,
Than in half your proud ladies that walk through
    the land.'

Words could but poorly help to convey an idea of the scorn with which these last lines were repeated. There might be a lesson to be learnt even in this nutshell of a Romany dwelling, and the pupils might be taken from the ranks of the proudest in the land and the teacher be no other than a gypsy's wife ; with only a wanderer's ideas of stability, and an outcast's views of morality.

" ' O you are a squire, and I'm a poor gypsy :
Both wealth and great beauty are at your command.
Some other fair beauty is won by false flattery,
And the poor gypsy wanderer is turned on the street.'

" ' But I'll tell you a secret, my virtuous young squire :
The gypsy will not to such misery be led.
The bright golden circle must be on my finger ;
Then through the churchyard is the way to my bed.'

" How this matter ended I did not stop to listen :
Some months passed away and winter drew near ;
I passed by a mansion, all was joy and splendour,
And the valleys they echoed with cheer after cheer ;
These words met my ear, and filled my heart with
    pleasure
" May they well prosper, and God be their guide.
Hail! hail! to the squire with these little treasures —
Long life to Selina, the dark gypsy bride.' "

ANGLO-ROMANY SONGS. 149

A mazurka-like tune accompanied these verses, and I was amused at watching the efforts of the little boy who was whittling over the stove making frantic efforts to keep time to the music with his penknife and bit of wood. I happened to break the point of my pencil whilst noting down the song, and he observed to his mother, "Her's *writer* is smashed." An enigmatic sentence, truly! but all gypsy-English is enigmatic.

The following is a well-known gypsy song of a very lively type, sung by the children at Upton Manor. Mr. George Smith, of Coalville, induced some of the more intelligent youngsters amongst them to repeat this one verse for him :—

> " Cush dearie Romany chile
> Delli in the moi,
> Sop me deary again Daddy
> If I can cawer * well."

The same day I visited old Jim Lee in his van at the end of Dirty Lane, Plaistow Marshes. This fine old man is not only the King of the famous Paraffin Lee tribe, but he is said to be the purest specimen of a gypsy at the present time to be found. I do not know

---

* Cawer-caw, the children of the gypsy tribes invariably speak of singing in this fashion.

whether any artist has immortalized this Romany monarch, but I should most certainly advise any one desirous of meeting with a perfect model of gypsy beauty to lose no time in transferring Jim Lee's features to canvas. The old man seemed quite pleased to give me all the information he could on the subject of the songs of the Romanies, and sent immediately for his cousin Job, who, he assured me, could sing well. Presently Job made his appearance, hobbling painfully over the muddy marsh-ground on two crutches. An equally fine-looking man, though of a less refined style, was this Job Lee. He wore a ragged blue guernsey and blue Tam-o'-Shanter cap, which served to add a touch of wildness to his already *farouche* appearance. The dexterity with which he mounted the narrow, unrailed steps which led to his kinsman's van was something to marvel at. He seemed to swing himself up by means of his crutches, and when he reached the top supported himself on the ledge of the small half-door, which always forms the entrance to a van dwelling, whilst he sang for me.

"This lady wants you to sing some Romany songs," said the old King.

"Can you rokra Romany, ranee?" ("Speak Romany, lady?") questioned Job.

I shook my head and told him "No;" but I understand it.

"Do you know this?" and to my delight he burst into the whittling song—

"Can you rokra Romany?
Can you play the bosh?
Can you jal adrey the staripen?
Can you chin the cost?"

"You'll not understand it, ranee," he said.

"Oh yes, I do; I have known it for a long time, but have never before heard the tune. Is it a great favourite amongst the gypsies?"

"Ay, that it is; they most sing it."

"Give us another, Job," broke in the old King.

"Where's your fiddle?"

"Do you play the bosh?" I asked the lame old vocalist; and the beaming smile with which my question was received showed me that I had, to use a familiar expression, "hit the right nail on the head."

He then sang me the following ballad, which I remember finding in Mr. Leland's book, "The Gypsies."

ROMANY BALLAD.

"Cosson kailyard corrum me morro sari,
Me gul ogalyach mir;
Rahet manent trasha moroch
Me tu sosti mo dīele."

"Coming from Galway tired and weary,
   I met a woman;
I'll go bail by this time to-morrow
   You'll have enough of me."

The following tent-song is also quoted by Mr. Leland:—

"GILLI OF A ROMANY JUVA."

"Dic at the Gargers,
   The Gargers round mandy!
Trying to lel my meripon,
   My meripon (meriben) away.

"I will care (kair) up to my chump (chongs),
   Up to my chump in rat,
All for my happy racher (raklo).
   My mush is lelled to sturribon staripen,
To sturribon, to sturribon;
   My mush is lelled to sturribon,
To the tan where mandy gins (jins)."

Translation of the foregoing, which is a gypsy woman's song:—

"Look at the Gorgios,
   The Gorgios around me!
Trying to take my life,
   My life away.

" I will wade up to my knees,
Up to my knees in blood,
All for my happy boy.
My husband's ta'en to prison,
To prison, to prison ;
My husband's ta'en to prison,
To the place of which I know."

I was told by several of the gypsies at Upton Park and Canning Town that this song is a great favourite amongst the gypsies of the South of England :—

"BANKS OF THE BEAUTIFUL SEVERN."

' On the banks of the beautiful Severn,
One ev'ning that long since has gone by,
We strayed till the clock struck eleven,
My own little Annie and I.
Her cheeks wore a blush like the roses,
Her breath like the hay newly mown,
Her eyes sparkled like the dew that reposes
n crystal-like drops on the foliag'd-clad thorn.

Chorus.
" On the banks of the beautiful Severn,
One evening that long since has gone by,
We stayed till the clock struck eleven,
My own little Annie and I.

"We strayed hand in hand together,
Our hearts beating high with true love;
We gazed on the stars as they twinkled,
And peep'd from the blue vault above.
She talked of the days of her childhood,
When gathering flowers on the lea;
And clasped her sweet hands as she nestled close to me,
And cried, 'Dearest, now do you love me?'

"We soon reached the door of her cottage,
Where Granny was waiting to see
The face of her own little darling
That was dearer than life unto me.
We stood at the gate for a moment,
Till Granny cried fiddle-de-dee;
She teazed me, and squeezed me, and pressed me so tight,
She kissed me, and wished me a very good-night."

This old jig and the two masques I found in a very old MS. book in the British Museum.

OLD ENGLISH GYPSY JIG.

THE GYPSIES' MASQUE.

GYPSY MASQUE.

It is very strange that Shakespeare never mentions the gypsies in any of his works; one would think they were the very people to have attracted his wonderfully roving pen, but I do not think with the exception of that sentence about "Bluff King Hal drinking with every tinker in his own tongue," there is one single allusion to them. Ben Jonson evidently thought them a musical people, as he intersperses his "Gypsy Masque" with so many songs and choruses.

SCOTCH GYPSY OR TINKLER SONGS.

"On Yeta's banks the vagrant gypsies place
Their turf-built cots; a sun-burnt, swarthy race!
From Nubian realms their tawny line they bring,
And their brown chieftain vaunts the name of king.
With loitering steps from town to town they pass,
Their lazy dames rocked on the panniered ass."
—*Poem on the Gypsies by* LEYDEN.

SCOTCH GYPSY OR TINKLER SONGS.

IN Scotland the gypsy tribe seems to have enjoyed some share of indulgence, for a writ of Privy Seal, dated 1594, supports John Faa, Lord and Earl of Little Egypt, in the execution of justice on his company and folk, conform to the laws of Egypt, and in punishing certain persons therein named who had rebelled, robbed him, absconded, and refused to return to Egypt. There is another writ in his favour from Mary Queen of Scots, 1553, and in 1554 he obtained a pardon for the murder of Nunan Small; so that it appears he had remained long in Scotland, and, perhaps, spent some time in England. From him this kind of strolling people received in Scotland the name of the Faa Gang. In later days they became known as Tinkers, and Kirk Yetholm, the chief *local* of the gypsies in Scotland, has one, if not more, of its streets named after them, such as "Tinkers' Row."

"Farewell to Kirk Yetholm and Cheviot's green
  hills,
Where gentle Queen Esther the gypsy throne fills.
Farewell to sweet Bowmont, whose bright water
  glides
Through thy dark glen where nature's wild beauty
  resides.

" The spell now is broken, thy glory is past;
Thy course, like the sun, disappears in the west.
Thy swart Eastern sons now no longer can rove
In freedom, to plunder, to fight, and to love.

" No longer the Faa at the head of his race
Returns to the palace with spoils of the chase;
In the smuggling foray no longer is heard
The song of wild mirth nor the clash of his swore

" Thy daughters who once, like the fairies of yore,
Danced round thy green knolls, now gamble no
  more;
Those dark eyes, whose glance set the heart all
  on flame,
No longer in Yetholm their empire proclaim."

In Scotland, perhaps, more than in any other country, the gypsies are divided into distinct tribes or clans, and the names of Winter, Gordon, and Baillie have long been recognized as those of the " Lordis of Littel Egypt."

Scotch fiction has incorporated much more of Romany lore than has the English. Sir Walter Scott has for ever rendered memorable the character of one gypsy woman, in that of Jean Gordon, the Meg Merrilies of "Guy Mannering;" and the pages of border history are full of the stirring deeds and thrilling adventures of the swarthy race. In some of the old volumes of *Blackwood's Magazine* are to be found some very interesting articles—"Recollections of Mark Macrabin, the Cameronian," in which there are many curious old Scotch saws and songs.

At Maybole over the Doon are some stepping stones still known as the Gypsy Steps, as they cross the river near Cassilis House, and were the means of Lady Cassilis escaping with the gypsy laddie, a theme which is often alluded to in Scotch ballads.—

"Yestreen I was a gentleman,
This night I am a tinkler;
Gae tell the lady o' this house
Come down to Sir John Sinclair."

The following is the version given by Finlay, in his collection of old Scottish ballads, of the "Gypsie Laddie," or "Johnny Faa."

"GYPSIE LADDIE."

" There came singers to Earl Cassilis gate,
    And O, but they sang bonnie ;
They sang sae sweet and sae complete,
    Till down came the Earl's lady.

" She came tripping down the stair,
    And all her maids before her ;
As soon as they saw her weel-faur'd face,
    They coost their glamourye o'er her.

" They gave her a' the gude sweetmeats,
    The nutmeg and the ginger ;
And she gied them a far better thing—
    Ten gowd rings off her finger.

" ' Come with me, my bonnie Jeanie Faa,
    O come with me, my dearie ;
For I do swear by the head o' my spear,
    Thy gude lord'll nae mair come near thee.'

"'Tak' from me my silken cloak,
  And bring me down my plaidie;
  For it is good, and good eneuch
  To follow a Gypsie Davy.'

"'Come saddle to me my horse,' he said;
 'Come saddle and make him ready;
  For I'll neither sleep, eat, nor drink
  Till I find out my lady.'

"They sought her up, they sought her down,
  They sought her thro' nations many;
  Till at length they found her out in bonny
      Abbeydale,
  Drinking wi' Gypsie Davy.

"'Rise, O rise! my bonnie Jeanie Faa,
  O rise and do not tarry:
  Is this the thing that ye promised to me,
  When at first I did thee marry?'

"They drunk her cloak, so did they her gown,
  They drunk her stockings and her shoon,
  They drunk the coat that was next her smock,
  And they pawned her pearled apron.

164 SCOTCH GYPSY OR TINKLER SONGS.

" They were sixteen clever men,
Suppose they were nae bonnie,
They are a' to be hanged on ae day,
For the stealing o' Earl Cassilis' lady.

" ' We are sixteen clever men,
One mother was a' our mother,
We are a' to be hanged on ae day,
For the stealing of a wanton lady.' "

Miss Burne also refers to this song as being sung under the title of "The Gypsy Laddie," by the gypsy children, in North Shropshire and Staffordshire.

THE GYPSY LADDIE.

SCOTCH GYPSY SONG.

THE LASS.

" ' O, haste ye, and come to our gate en',
And solder the stroup o' my lady's pan:
My lord's away to hunt the doe,'
Quo' the winsome lass o' Gallowa'.

THE TINKER.

" 'I ha'e a pan o' my ain to clout,
Before I can solder your lady's stroup,
And ye maun bide, my mettle to blaw,
My winsome lass o' Gallowa'.
Now, wad ye but leave your gay lady
And carry the tinkling tool wi' me,
And lie on kilns, on clean ait straw,
My winsone lass o' Gallowa'.'

THE LASS.

" 'The fingers that starch my lady's frills
Never could carry your tinkling tools;
Ye're pans wad grime my neck o' snaw,'
Quo' the winsome lass o' Gallowa'.
Her hair in hanks of golden thread
O'er her milk-white shoulders was loosely spread;
And her bonny blue een blinked love below,
My winsome lass o' Gallowa'.

THE TINKER.

" I took her by the jimpy waist,
And her lips stood tempting to be kist;
But whether I kiss'd them well or no,
Ye may ask the lass o' Gallowa'.'

THE LASS.

"'Now quat the grip, thou gypsy loon,
Thou hast touzzl'd me till my breath is done,
And my lady will fret frae bower to ha','
Quo' the winsome lass o' Gallowa'.

THE TINKER.

"'Ye've coupit the soldering-pan, my lass,
And ye have scaled my clinks o' brass,
And my gude spoon caams ye've split in twa,
My winsome lass o' Gallowa'.

The English gypsies seemed to have had no great love for the Scotch tinklers, and it is very rare to find an instance of any intermarriage. "Nasty Scotch Faws" the English Romanies call them; only partially gypsy, "half-and-halfs," or "a thimbleful of Romany to a bucket of Gorgio blood." Sometimes a Scoto-Romany will unloose his tongue and become jovial under the English-Romany canvas, but only occasionally, and then under the potent influence of bourri-zimmins (snail soup), or hotchi-witchy (baked hedgehog), washed down with a bumper of whisky or rum and water, for the Romany byword applies well to the Scottish tinker—"A hedgehog will open when he is wet." They are all patriotic these roadside Arabs of the Land o' Cakes, a fact that may probably be accounted for by their being so much mixed with native blood ; but, like ill-used mongrel curs, they have a seeming deep mistrust of all mankind ; and though possessed of a fund of Border tale and song, it is not an easy matter to induce one of them to impart any information, even should the interlocutor be capable of rókering Romanes (talking Romany).

This lay of the Reedwater minstrel, on Will Allan, is perhaps worthy a place amongst a collection of the songs of the tribe he so worthily adorned :—

" A stalwart tinkler wight was he,
  And weel could mend a pot or pan,
An' deftly weel could thraw a flee,
  An' neatly weave the willow wan.

" An' sweetly wild were Allan's strains,
  An' mony a jig an' reel he blew,
Wi' merry lilts he charm'd the swains,
  Wi' barbèd spear the otter slew," etc.

Jamie Allan, his son, the celebrated Northumbrian piper, died in the jail, or "staripen," at Morpeth, Northumberland, whither his manifold crimes had led him. For some time Jamie held the post of Piper to the Duke of Northumberland, but he was too much the unprincipled vagabond, " the regular, rollicking,

168 SCOTCH GYPSY OR TINKLER SONGS.

Romany," to be retained long in such a capacity. Jamie agreed with the spirit of Addison's words—

"When liberty is gone, life grows insipid, and has lost its relish."

Flying one day from some pursuers, he dropped from the summit of a very high wall, and received a severe cut on his right hand in doing so. He exclaimed, as he turned upon his followers, "Ye ha'e spoiled the best pipe hand in Britain." The story of the faithful love Jamie received during the whole of his disreputable career, from his gypsy wife, is one of great pathos. One almost feels inclined to wonder at fidelity, or indeed at the charm which could have led to its origin; but then we may question with Byron—

"Why did she love him? curious fool! be still.
Is human love the growth of human will?"

The following is a tinkler's song, sometimes attributed to Yetholm :—

TINKLER'S SONG.

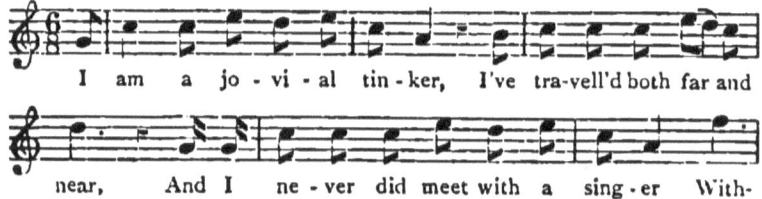

I am a jo-vi-al tin-ker, I've tra-vell'd both far and near, And I ne-ver did meet with a sing-er With-

SCOTCH GYPSY OR TINKLER SONGS. 169

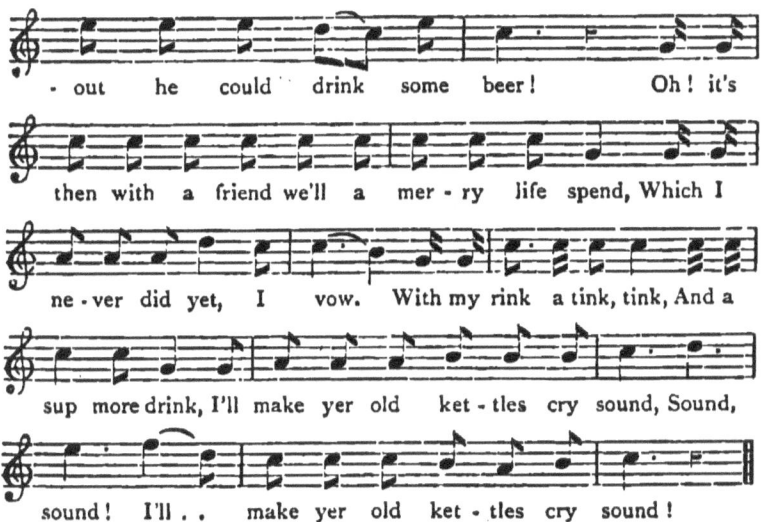

- out he could drink some beer! Oh! it's
then with a friend we'll a mer-ry life spend, Which I
ne-ver did yet, I vow. With my rink a tink, tink, And a
sup more drink, I'll make yer old ket-tles cry sound, Sound,
sound! I'll .. make yer old ket-tles cry sound!

The following pretty little slang Romany song hails also from the Land o' Burns, and was sent me by Mr. George Smith, of Coalville, who may safely claim to be the gypsy's best friend :—

> " Shela, Shela,
> Shela gang a' rue,
> Shela gang a'
> Ricki, dicki,
> Shela gaggie o ;
> Shela gang a',
> Lagghi dagghi.
> Sweet malori
> Sweet Jamie's the lad
> That I'll gang wi'.

"I'll due my petticoatie,
I'll dye it red,
And wi' my bonnie laddie
I'll beg my bread;
And wi' my bonnie laddie
I'll beg my bread.
Sweet Jamie's the lad
That I'm gaen wi'."

To thoroughly understand the Scottish gypsies or tinklers, there can be no better medium than Walter Simson's "History of the Gypsies." Their many curious customs, manners, etc., are most exhaustively and interestingly treated in this work. Speaking of their singing, the author says, "As far as I can judge, from the few and short specimens which I have myself heard, and had reported to me, the subjects of the songs of the Scottish gypsies (I mean those composed by themselves) are chiefly their plunderings, their robberies, and their sufferings. The numerous and deadly conflicts which they had among themselves, also, afforded them themes for the exercise of their muse. My father, in his youth, often heard them singing songs wholly in their own language. They appear to have been very fond of our ancient Border marauding songs which celebrate the daring exploits of the lawless freebooters on the frontiers of Scotland and England. They were constantly singing these compositions among themselves. The song composed on Hughie Graeme, the horse-stealer, published in the second volume of Sir Walter Scott's "Border Minstrelsy," was a great favourite with the tinklers. As this is completely to the taste of a gypsy, I will here insert it, as affording a good specimen of that description of song in the singing of which they take great delight. It will also serve to show the peculiar cast of mind of the gypsies.

"HUGHIE THE GRAEME."

"Gude Lord Scroope's to the hunting gane,
   He has ridden o'er moss and muir,
And he has grippit Hughie the Graeme,
   For stealing o' the bishop's mare.

"'Now, good Lord Scroope, this may not be!
   Here hangs a broadsword by my side;
And if that thou canst conquer me,
   The matter it may soon be tried.'

"'I ne'er was afraid of a traitor-thief;
   Although thy name be Hughie the Graeme,
I'll make thee repent thee of thy deeds,
   If God but grant me life and time.'

"' Then do your worst now, good Lord Scroope,
   And deal your blows as hard as you can;
It shall be tried, within an hour,
   Which of us two is the better man.'

" But as they were dealing their blows so free,
   And both so bloody at the time,
Over the moss came ten yeoman so tall,
   All for to take brave Hughie the Graeme.

"' Then they hae grippit Hughie the Graeme,
   And brought him up through Carlisle town;
The lassies and lads stood on the walls,
   Crying, ' Hughie the Graeme, thou'se ne'er
      [gae down.'

" Then hae they chosen a jury of men,
   The best that were in Carlisle town;
And twelve of them cried out at once,
   ' Hughie the Graeme, thou must gae down.'

" Then up bespak him gude Lord Hume,
   As he sat by the judge's knee—
"' Twenty white owsen, my gude lord,
   If you'll grant Hughie the Graeme to me.'

" ' O no, O no, my gude Lord Hume!
    For sooth and sae it manna be;
For were there but three Graeme's of the name
    They suld be hanged a' for me.'

" "Twas up and spake the gude Lady Hume,
    As she sat by the judge's knee—
' A peck of white pennies, my gude lord judge,
    If you'll grant Hughie the Graeme to me.'

" ' O no, O no, my gude Lady Hume!
    For sooth and so it must na be;
Were he but the one Graeme of the name,
    He suld be hanged high for me.'

" ' If I be guilty,' said Hughie the Graeme,
' Of me my friends shall have small talk;'
And he has louped fifteen feet and three,
    Though his hands they were tied behind his back.

" He looked over his left shoulder,
    And for to see what he might see;
There was he aware of his auld father,
    Came tearing his hair most piteouslie.

"'O! hald your tongue, my father,' he says,
    And see that ye dinna weep for me!
For they may ravish me o' my life,
    But they canna banish me fro' Heavin hie.

"'Fare ye well, fair Maggie, my wife!
    The last time we came ower the muir,
'Twas thou bereft me of my life,
    And wi' the Bishop thou play'd the whore.

"'Here, Johnie Armstrang, take thou my sword,
    That is made o' the metal sae fine;
And when thou comest to the English side,
    Remember the death of Hughie the Graeme.'"

Referring to the gyysies' disinclination to enter the services, Mr. Simson narrates several instances of them voluntarily mutilating themselves. Rather than become a soldier or a sailor, a gypsy would sacrifice one or two fingers, or even an arm or leg; and mothers were known to deprive their little ones of their digits to ensure their freedom from military service. A tinkler's song, to the tune of "Clout the Caudron," is descriptive of this horror of enlisting

"My bonnie lass, I work in brass,
    A tinkler is my station;
I've travelled round all Christian ground
    In this my occupation.
I've ta'en the gold, an' been enroll'd
    In many a noble squadron;
But vain they searched when off I marched
    To go and clout the caudron."

Gypsies sometimes voluntarily join the Navy as musicians. Here their vanity has a field for conspicuous display; for a good fifer on board of a man-o'-war, in accompanying certain work with his music, is equal to the services of ten men. There were some gypsy musicians in the fleet at Sebastopol. But, generally speaking, gypsies are like cats—not very fond of the water. The Scottish gypsies have, doubtless, an oral literature, like their brethren in other countries. It would be strange indeed if they did not rank as high in that respect as many of the barbarous tribes in the world. People so situated, with no written language, are wonderfully apt at picking up and retaining any composition that contains poetry and music to which oral literature is chiefly confined. In that respect their faculties, like those of the blind, are sharpened by the wants which others do not experience in indulging a feeling common to all mankind.

Whilst in the north of England lately, I contemplated a visit to Yetholm for the purpose of seeking for any tinkler songs which might be found there; but I was dissuaded from the idea on being told by a very good authority on gypsy matters that there are now no genuine tinklers to be found in the place. All the gypsies of Yetholm have become respectable farm-labourers, small shopkeepers, etc., and if any pursue their old calling, namely, that of tinkering, they do so under widely different circumstances. They have neat cottages, proper appliances, and all that is requisite for making out of it a comfortable living. The bonny children playing, where in days gone by their parents in true tinkler disorder had rioted away the sunny hours of their life's morning, bear the traces of their gypsy origin in their tawny faces, now bright and clean, and set off by tidy frocks and coats where there had been only rags and tatters ; the old people carefully tended, and dozing away their declining years either in their chairs by the chimney corner, or in the sunshine out in the porch watching their grandchildren at their games, thinking of their own rough tent-life in their young days, it may be even looking back with pleasure on what has gone before, it may be quietly resigned to the end which cannot be far off, for—

"Each day brings less summer cheer,
  Crimps* more our ineffectual spring;
And something earlier every year,
  Our singing birds take wing."

I cannot close a chapter on Scotch gypsy songs without quoting some from Sir Walter Scott's novel, "Guy Mannering." Meg Merrilies' wild verses need no particularly keen imagination to wed them to the music we know to be suited to them. Her voice Sir Walter describes as being too shrill for a man, and too low for a woman. One of the songs runs thus:—

"Canny moment, lucky fit,
  Is the lady lighter yet?
Be it lad or be it lass,
  Sign wi' cross, and sain wi' mass."

And another, a charm, set to a wild tune:—

"Trefoil, vervain, John's-wort dill,
  Hinders witches of their will;
Weel is them, that weel may
  Fast upon St. Andrew's day.

* North Country term for "shortens."

"Saint Bride and her brat,
Saint Colme and his cat,
Saint Michael and his spear,
Keep the house frae reif and wear."

And then there is the strange gypsy spinning song :—

"Twist ye, twine ye! even so
Mingle shades of joy and woe,
Hope, and fear, and peace, and strife
In the thread of human life.

"While the mystic twist is spinning,
And the infant's life beginning,
Dimly seen through twilight bending,
Lo, what varied shapes attending!

"Passions wild, and follies vain,
Pleasures soon exchanged for pain ;
Doubt, and jealousy, and fear
In the magic dance appear.

"Now they wax, and now they dwindle,
Whirling with the whirling spindle.
Twist ye, twine ye! even so
Mingle human bliss and woe."

And lastly, one of those strange prayers, or rather spells, which in some parts of Scotland and the

North of England are used by the vulgar and ignorant to speed the passage of a parting spirit, like the tolling of the bell in Catholic days. This dismal song is accompanied with a slow rocking motion of the body to and fro, as if to keep time with the rhythm.

The words run nearly thus :—

"Wasted, weary, wherefore stay,
Wrestling thus with earth and clay?
From the body pass away;—
  Hark! the mass is singing.

"From thee doff thy mortal weed,
Mary Mother be thy speed,
Saints to help thee at thy need;—
  Hark! thy knell is ringing.

"Fear not snow-drift driving fast,
Sleet, or hail, or levin blast;
Soon the shroud shall lap thee fast,
And the sleep on thee be cast
  That shall ne'er know waking.

"Haste thee, haste thee, to be gone,
Earth flits fast, and time draws on,
Gasp thy gasp, and groan thy groan,
  Day is near the breaking."

SONGS OF THE BOHÉMIENS;

OR,

FRENCH GYPSY SONGS.

"He renders all his lore
In numbers wild as dreams."
—EMERSON.

"A monarchy tempered by song."—CHAMPFORD.

SONGS OF THE BOHÉMIENS.

THE gypsies, or Bohémiens as they are called in France, do not open up that wide field of song one would expect in the country of the troubadour. Gypsy legend finds a cradle-land in Normandy and Brittany, and in the mountainous district of Auvergne, but gypsy music has either never made a home for itself amongst the light-hearted peasantry of the country, or, if it has found that home, is unwilling to leave it or to permit strangers to seek it there. A few specimens of the tambourine songs in vogue many years ago amongst the Bohémiens all over France I have been able to meet with, and also some of the songs of the Romanies of Auvergne, styled Perigourdines.

The following is a sample of the former:—

FRENCH GYPSY TAMBOURINE SONG.

"Tambouriça, mon passe-temps;
Archet, ma douce joie;

Assez longtemps tu as nourri ma faim,
Désaltéré ma soif,
Tu as attiré les filles à la fenêtre,
Tu as allumé d'amour leurs visages.
Tambouriça, mon passe-temps ;
Archet, ma douce joie ;
Hélas ! j'ai perdu les jours et l'année,
A chanter sous les fenêtres de Meïra ;
Meïra ne veut même pas me regarder."

Translation.

" Tambourine, my joy in leisure ;
Thou bow, my sweetest, sweetest treasure ;
How oft hast thou my hunger fed,
My burning thirst to water led,
And to the windows drawn the maids,
And crowned with love their silken braids.
Tambourine, my joy in leisure ;
Thou bow, my sweetest, sweetest treasure ;
Alas ! what days and years I've spent
In singing under Meïra's windows,
And Meïra has never a look on me sent."

Most of us have heard of the gypsy bird legend, an account of which appeared in the Paris *Figaro*,

OR, FRENCH GYPSY SONGS. 185

October, 1872. Speaking of the death of a gypsy woman belonging to a tribe encamped in the Rue Duhesme, after relating various ceremonies performed outside the tent, the author goes on to explain that all the gypsies present formed a circle round the dying woman. A man, who appeared to be the chief of the tribe, then came into the middle of the circle holding a bird in his hand, which he placed near the mouth of the young woman. In about a quarter of an hour the gypsy uttered a cry and expired. Her companions carried back the body into the tent, and let loose the bird. This curious ceremony was performed with the view of introducing the soul of the young woman into the bird thus carrying out the Chinese idea of the transmigration of souls.

The following is a specimen of the Perigourdines :—

PERIGOURDINE (GYPSIES OF AUVERGNE).

The sentiments of the song which I give next are totally at variance with those generally expressed by the Romany class.

GYPSIES' SONG (AUVERGNE).

Par - tons vite et tôt, Ga - gnons la prai - ri - e; Pour l'ou vrage il faut Par - tir vite et tôt. Tra - vail et gai - té Pro - lon - gent la vi - e; Tra - vail et gai - té Don - nent la san - té.

"Let us go quickly and soon,
We must get to the meadows,
For work it is necessary that we
Should be off quickly and soon.
Work and gaiety prolong our life;
Work and gaiety bring us health."

We are all probably familiar with Ouida's most poetical descriptions of music; and amongst the many characters she has sketched for us there is not one that lovers of music find more interesting to follow through the intricate mazes of their eventful lives than that of the wandering Tricotrin, a gypsy in all but the name. A life as free as that of the birds, with a heart as generous as his purse was niggardly, a soul as full of music as his fingers of dexterity, Tricotrin was the life and light of every village *fête* from the shores of the tideless Mediterranean to the stormbound coast of Normandy; and Ouida best describes his wonderful genius when she says of it, "That music which had given its hymn for the vintage feast of the Loire, and which had brought back the steps of the suicide from the river brink in the darkness of the Paris night, which sovereigns could not command, and which held peasants entranced by its spell." The French gypsy vagrant, with his favourite monkey, "Bébé," on his back, his beloved violin in his hand, bringing sunshine where the shadows deepest fell amongst the poor labourers of the richest province of France, is a picture one reverts to with a feeling of something that is as near akin to the admiration one feels for some hero as may be. A verse from Leland's poem, "'The Bohemian," comes to my memory as I write, which better pleads the gypsy cause than anything I can say of it.

"E'en outcasts may have heart and feeling,
    The blackest wild Tzigan be true,
And love, like light in dungeons stealing,
    Though bars be there, will still break through."

In France, before the Revolution, there were but few gypsies, for the obvious reason that every gypsy who could be apprehended fell a sacrifice to the police. "I would suppose that these severe edicts of the French would drive the gypsies to adopt the costume and manners of the other inhabitants. In this way they would disappear from the public eye. The officers of justice would, of course, direct their attention to what would be understood to be gypsies— that is, tented gypsies, or those who professed their ways, such as fortune-telling, etc. I have met with a French gypsy in the streets of New York engaged as a dealer in candy."—*Grellmann.*

It must be reluctantly granted that in two countries in Europe the costumes and manners of the gypsies are to a certain extent romantic. The French Bohémiens are merely ragged tramps, so sharply looked after by the gendarmerie that they are powerless to do much mischief. Yet, in spite of this, the profession, if one may so call it, of fortune-telling is largely pursued by the Bohémiens; and amidst the rich verdant country of sunny and sun-loved France, Crabbe's picture of the encampment of the fortune teller is often realized :—

. . . "A hollow on the left appeared,
And there a gypsy tribe their tent had reared.
'Twas open spread to catch the morning sun,
And they had now their early meal begun,
When two brown boys just left their grassy seat
The early traveller with their prayers to greet.
Within, the father, who from fences nigh
Had brought the fuel for the fire's supply,
Watch'd now the feeble blaze, and stood dejected by.
On rugged rug, just borrow'd from the bed,
And by the hand of coarse indulgence fed,
In dirty patchwork negligently dressed,
Reclined the wife, an infant at her breast;
In her wild face some touch of grace remained,
Of vigour palsied, and of beauty stain'd,
Her blood-shot eyes on her unheeding mate
Were wrathful turn'd, and seem'd her wants to state,
Cursing his tardy aid ; her mother there
With gypsy state engross'd the only chair—
Solemn and dull her look ; with such she stands
And reads the milkmaid's fortune in her hands,
Tracing the lines of life ; assumed through years,
Each feature now the steady falsehood wears."

The following rather naughty little song used to be a great favourite amongst the French gypsies. I do not think it is known by any particular title.

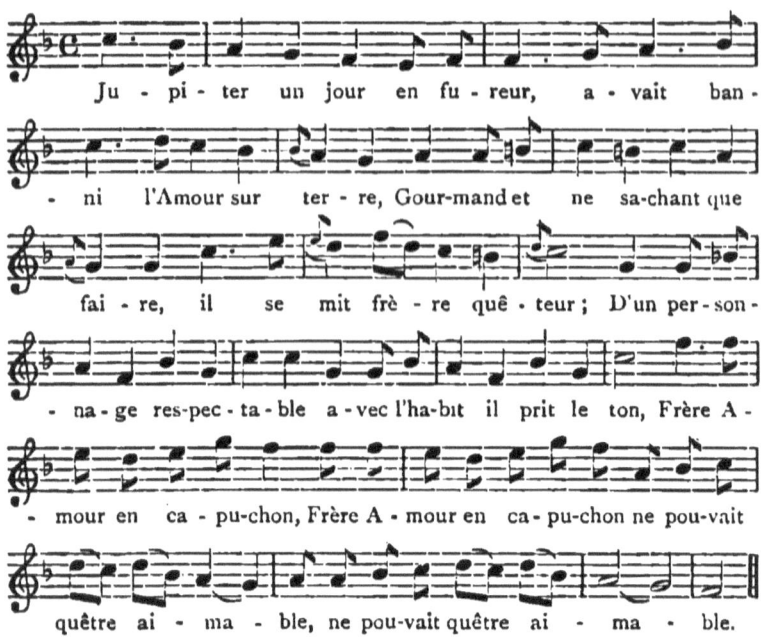

Ju - pi - ter un jour en fu - reur, a - vait ban - ni l'Amour sur ter - re, Gour-mand et ne sa-chant que fai - re, il se mit frè - re quê - teur; D'un per-son - na - ge res - pec - ta - ble a - vec l'ha-bit il prit le ton, Frère A - mour en ca - pu - chon, Frère A - mour en ca - pu - chon ne pou-vait quêtre ai - ma - ble, ne pou-vait quêtre ai - ma - ble.

" Voici le petit Cupidon
   Courant le monde à l'aventure,
   Le dieu qui soumet la nature
   Est réduit à l'abandon.
   À la porte d'un monastère,
   Il arriva tout fatigué,
' Faites-moi la charité [*bis*]
   Je suis dans la misère.' [*bis*]

"Aux cris du jeune séducteur
Une nonne vint à la porte ;
Voyant Cupidon de la sorte,
La pitié gagna son cœur.
' Pour vous délasser de la route,
Mon Frère, entrez dans la maison,
Prenez-moi par mon cordon,' [*bis*]
' Ma Sœur, je n'y voit goutte.' [*bis*]

"Sans le savoir la pauvre Agnès
Mit le loup dans la bergerie,
Et son innocence chérie
Va s'envoler pour jamais,
Frère Amour eut tant d'éloquence
Qu'il parvint à la convertir,
Lui fit aimer le plaisir [*bis*]
En prêchant pénitence. [*bis*]

" Bientôt le petit Cupidon,
Passa de celulle en celulle,
A Sœur Brigide, à Sœur Ursule
Il va présentant son tronc,
Partout il reçoit mainte Aumône,
Et pour le dimanche suivant
Chaque nonne du Couvent [*bis*]
Le recommande au Prone. [*bis*]

"L'Amour en Frocque était charmant,
Mais il n'était pas moins volage,
Je vais achever mon voyage
Leur dit-il d'un ton dolent.
'Ah! quel tourment, Ah! quel supplice
Vous nous quittez, petit fripon,
Laissez-nous votre cordon, [*bis*]
Mes Sœurs, Dieu vous bénisse. [*bis*]

"'Juste ciel, le voilà parti!'
Dit l'Abesse fondant en larmes,
Ah! grand Dieu, qu'il avait de charme,
Que de plaisir il nous fit.
Du cordon le St. exercise
Réchauffait la dévotion;
'Vite à son intention [*bis*]
Récitons notre office.'" [*bis*]

There are, I believe, several versions of this naïve chanson. This one was taken down from the lips of an old French gypsy man, who chuckled very delightedly over the repeating of it. I am half afraid to risk an English version, such lines as,

"Sans le savoir la pauvre Agnès
Mit le loup dans la bergerie,"

would lose decidedly by translation; as would also, "L'amour en Frocque était charmant."

A very slight knowledge of French will suffice for a comprehension of the verses, so I will not attempt what would only detract from their interest.

FRENCH GYPSY DANCE.
(SIXTEENTH CENTURY.)

FRENCH GYPSY SONG (AUVERGNE).

The following, known as the "Air du Prix," is not essentially a ballad of Bohemia, as many who are acquainted with French songs will vouch for, but it is often to be heard trolled out by the lips of the lazy *insouciant* vagabonds as they roam the country lanes

194   SONGS OF THE BOHÉMIENS;

and gay towns of *la belle France.* It has just the impudence about it that would be likely to make it a welcome addition to a Bohemian's *répertoire.*

"AIR DU PRIX."
(Sung by the French Gypsies.)

Tour-ner ain-si la tê-te, et cau-ser à part soi, ce-la n'est pas hon-nê-te; mon- sieur, re-gar-dez-moi, mon-sieur, mon-sieur, re-gar-dez- moi. Vous ê-tes, je le vois, em- bar-ras-sé du choix! oh! oui, je le de-vi-ne; en re-gar-dant Jus-ti-ne, vous pen-sez à Pau- li-ne; et vous res-tez rê-veur; mon-sieur, mon- sieur, mon-trez-vous, mon-trez vous con-nois- sieur, mon-trez-vous, mon-trez-vous con-nois-seur.

FRENCH GYPSY SONG.

(Known as "Air Tendre.")

English version of " Air du Prix."
" Thus to turn one's head
And talk apart
Is not gallant, sir.
Look at me, sir ;
Sir, look at me.
I see you feel embarrassed
How to make a choice
In looking at Justine.
You think of Pauline,
And you pause and dream.
Oh sir, show yourself a *connoisseur ;*
Sir, show yourself a *connoisseur.*"

English version of " Air Tendre."
" Echoes of these forests, who have so often
Repeated the vows made to me by Celimene,
And you birds who sang in these woods,
Learn my mortal trouble.
The ungrateful creature has made me weep;
She receives the homage of another lover.
Echoes, echoes, repeat my sorrows
To the faithless one; to the faithless one,
Echoes, repeat my sorrows."

The drinking-song, or " Air à Boire," which I give next, is somewhat coarse in sentiment, but, as I believe it to be a genuine Romany chorus, I insert it.

OR, FRENCH GYPSY SONGS.

"AIR À BOIRE."
(Gipsy Drinking Chorus.)

This so-called "Chanson Nouvelle" I found in an old MS. book, the date of which, together with the words of this particular song, were entirely obliterated by the hand of Time.

"CHANSON NOUVELLE" (BOHÉMIENNE).

This strange little ballet is attributed to the Bohémiens:—

"Son Louys souspire
Après ses appas,
Que veut-elle dire
De ne venir pas.

"S'il ne la possède
Il s'en va mourir ;
Donnons-y remède,
Allons le guérir.

"Assemblons, Marie,
Les yeux à vos yeux
Nostre bergerie
N'en vaudra que mieux.

"Hastons le voyage,
Le siècle Doré
En ce mariage
Nous est assuré."

"J'ay beau boire sans cesse" ("I may as well drink without stopping") is another of these favourite *thirst songs* of the Bohémiens of the last century, the tune is as follows:—

"J'AY BEAU BOIRE SANS CESSE."

"J'ay beau boire sans cesse,
La soif toujours me presse ;
Je suis charmé quand j'aperçois
Que l'on verse du vin pour *moy*.

"Dans votre humeur coquette
Vous me contez fleurette.
Ah ! que vous seriez obligeant
Si vous me comptiez de l'argent."

"I may as well drink without stopping,
Since my thirst never leaves me;
I am charmed when I perceive
That any one pours out wine for me.

"In your mischievous coquetry
You ask the flower-petals of my love,
Ah ! how obliging you would be
If you would count me out some money."

I read in a French novel (whose name and author I have entirely forgotten) a charming description of some gypsies encamped near the château where the scene of the book was laid, and this song was given as one that the writer heard sung by them. There is a legend told in Auvergne which resembles very closely the Scotch story of Earl Cassilis and the gypsy laddie, which has been handed down to posterity in prose and verse, and which in the latter form I have alluded to in another part of this little work. The French romance was that of a beautiful young lady, a notary's daughter, who, so the harsh historians have it, fell in love and ran away with a gypsy whose beauty was undeniable, but whose moral qualities were—well, we'll say in process of formation. The notary of course objected, and to prevent any *esclandre* in the shape of a return to the parental shelter, he sold his practice and his patrimony and left the country. This song which follows was the one sung beneath his beloved's casement by the bold Romany, the night she fled with him :—

"Quand je vous dis que la nuit et le jour
Je meurs pour vous d'amour,
Vous ne me croyez pas,
Mademoiselle D'Angla,
Vous ne me croyez pas,
Mademoiselle D'Angla.
Votre esprit est quinteux comme une mule,
Et cependant je suis si ridicule
Que votre corps
Fait mes transports."

" When I tell you that night and day
I die for love of you,
You won't believe me,
Mademoiselle D'Angla ;
You won't believe me,
Mademoiselle D'Angla.
Your soul is as stubborn as a mule,
And all the same I am ridiculous enough
To let your form
Be my delight."

"QUAND JE VOUS DIS QUE LA NUIT ET LE JOUR."

I have no words to the next, which was sent to me as a well-known " Air des Bohémiens " by a very eminent musical author in France, and with a few words to tell me that it had been taken down by himself from some of the wanderers :—

"AIR DES BOHÉMIENS."

THE ZIGEŬNER OR GYPSIES OF THE VATERLAND.

" Come, then, a song ; a winding, gentle song,
To lead me to sleep."
—BEDDOES.

THE ZIGEŬNER.

Hermann Mendel, in his invaluable "Musikalisches Conversations-Lexikon," devotes a few pages to the Zigeŭner. He refers to the use of the hackbut and cymbals amongst the gypsies in former times.

At the present day the hackbut is a favourite instrument with the Romanies in Hungary. This hackbut, or *cobza*, is struck with bells, and produces a most penetrating sound. Bárna Mihaly, a gypsy, became so proficient a performer on it that he was given the name of the "Magyar Orpheus" by Count Cschaky. Mendel intersperses all his remarks on the German gypsies with so many on those of Transylvania, that I am tempted to agree with a great authority on Romany lore, who told me that the discipline of the Vaterland is too severe to admit of these lawless people finding tolerance, or even shelter, in the country. Certainly, there have been many books written on the Zigeŭner; but there is little to be learnt as to their music. Peter Cornelius' work only treats of the Hungarian gypsy music.* Graf-

---

* "Die Zigeŭner ŭnd ihre Musik in Ungarn."

fŭnder has collected some few German gypsy songs, The following is a specimen of them :—

ROMANY (GERMAN) SONG.

"Gader wela!
Gader Stela!
Ab, Miro tschabo ste!
I tarni romni dschalu, Mangel;
I puri romni balo póp Priesterwela.

"I tarni romni har i rosa,
I puri romni har i dschamba,
I tarni romni weli tarno rom,
I puri romni weli puro rom."

"Woher kommt er,
Woher springt er,
Aŭf mein Sohn und spring!
Die jŭnge Fraŭ geht, betteln (geht bettelt),
Die alte Fraŭ hinterm Ofen riestert.

"Die jŭnge Fraŭ gleich einer Rose,
Die alte Fraŭ gleich einer Kröte,
Die jŭnge Fraŭ krigt einen jŭngen Mann,
Die alte Fraŭ krigt einen alten Mann."

One thing Mendel admits with regard to all gypsy music, and that is the perfection the rare gift of improvisation attains amongst them. I believe Graffünder is the only writer on the gypsies who alludes to the strange adaptibility of the Romany tongue to musical setting. He says, "Die Sprache ist wohlklingend, und dem Gesange sehr günstig." Graffünder several times mentions the Scandinavian gypsies; but then his book on the Zigeuner was published in 1835, when there were probably to be found tribes of Romanies in these northern lands. To-day they are almost unknown, and, with the exception of two so-called Swedish gypsy tunes, which I found in a very old volume of Norske melodies, I have never come across any mention of music pertaining to the wanderers in Scandinavia.

SWEDISH GYPSY SONG.

SWEDISH GYPSY SONG.

INDIAN, SOUTH AMERICAN, AND ARABIAN GYPSY SONGS AND DANCE TUNES.

"Where should this music be,
In the air or the earth?"
—SHAKESPEARE.

INDIA.

IT would appear that music is generally cultivated in Hindostan; and in Central India, according to Sir John Malcolm, most of the villages have attached to them men and women of the Nutt or Bamallee tribes, who appear to be a kind of wandering gypsies, and have attached to them rude musicians and minstrels, whose music and songs form the chief entertainment of the peasantry. These musicians are divided into two classes, Chârims and Bhâts; they boast of a Celestial origin,* and exercise an influence of a very powerful description over the people.

The very charming Hindu air which follows I heard sung by an English gypsy-woman almost note for note as I found it in a valuable book on " Hindu Music from various Authors, compiled by Sourindro Mohun

* Can these be the "Heavenly Zincali" spoken of by James Russell Lowell in his poem of " The Changling? "

" A troup of wandering angels
Stole my little daughter away;
Or, perhaps, those heavenly Zincali
But loosed the hampering strings," etc.

Tagore; for private circulation only. Calcutta, 1875." This song is so plaintive and so pretty that I could wish some of our gifted nineteenth-century song-makers would re-set it in a more worthy shrine of harmony. I give the original Hindu words as they are to be found in the work before referred to.

" Kurna na päee bāt
　Ab. myn.　Peea soo jeea ke bat
　Oodowjee! tahreean, myn bulaeen leongi ho!
　Mohe le'chulo oonhen ke pas."

HINDU AIR, "KURNA NA PÄEE BĀT."

English Words.

" I could not speak with him, those fondest words
Which I had treasured up to tell ;
My streaming eyes were dim with weary tears,
Which then, alas! unheeded fell.
Rude blows the bitter wind, cold is the driving rain,
Nor place I find to dwell ;
Ah me! from them. unkind, no pitying word ;
No sheltering love I find.

" Ah! now I vainly cry,
 Dear Lord, dear heart so fondly loved,
Thou wouldst not see me lie
So desolate, nor fail that love so truly proved.
Rest, rest! oh breaking heart ;   [mov'd.
Peace cometh now to thee, that nought had ever
Ah! why delay thy dart ?   [part.
Kind death, take me to him, that never more we

The following are dance tunes used by the Nutts or Indian gypsies :—

DANCE TUNE OF THE INDIAN GYPSIES.

DANCE TUNE OF THE NUTTS.

This Bengalee song is a great favourite amongst Indian gypsies:—

"Nock erbesor Jeelee mille
Poteer gulla doorea Koonja
Choola danntee hassia Naaloo
Rangonee gwalia naalo."

The songs of a nation go a great way towards developing its domestic practices, rites, and ceremonies; as also its habits of life. Thus the allowed insignificance of the female sex in the idea of a Hindoo, the contempt in which they are generally held, leave very considerable effects on their poetry. In Hindostan the fair sex are the first to woo, and the man after much courting yields. We must make all allowance for this Oriental prejudice which assigns the active part of amorous intercourse to the female, and makes the mistress seek the lover, not the lover his mistress. In compositions of this country, therefore, love and desire, hope and passion, are first felt in the female bosom, and evinced by her pathetic exclamations.

BENGALEE SONG.

SONGS OF THE CHINGANEROS.

In South America there is a peculiar race of wandering Creole minstrels, whose habits and even whose appellations strikingly resemble those of the Zinganees, or Eastern gypsies. They claim for themselves pure

Indian descent; but this is denied by the aborigines. They are all good dancers and musicians, and, above all, fortune-tellers, supposed sorcerers, and *improvisatori*. These people are held in utter contempt and abhorrence by all true Indians; and not even the meanest tribes among them will hold any intercourse with the Chinganeros, whom they consider degraded by their buffoonery to the level of monkeys. Their agility and humour, nevertheless, render their occasional visits always welcome to the light-hearted Creoles; and even the supercilious Spaniards deigned at times to relax from their haughty gravity, and to smile at their unpolished gambols. We may judge of their power as minstrels by the two following examples:—

"LA MONTONÉRA."

"Montonéra soy señoras,
 Yo no niego mi nacion,
 Mas vale ser Montonéra
 Que no Porteno pintor;
 Montonéra, en Buenos Ayres,
 Por las pampas he pasado;
 Montonéra por las nieves,
 De las Andes he baxado.

"En su curso por el cielo,
Quien atajará al Lucéro?
Mas atreve quien pretiendo
Atajar al Montonéra.
Libres vuelan los Condores
Por la cana Cordilléra;
Y no menos por los valles,
Libre va la Montonéra."

Translation.

"A Montonéra's life I lead—
I'll ne'er disown the name,
Though village maids and city dames
May lightly hold our fame.
From Buenos Ayres' boundless plains,
The Montonéra comes.
And o'er the mighty Andes' heights
In liberty she roams.

"What hand e'er tried in empty space
To arrest the morning star?
The Montonéra's freeborn mind
To enslave is harder far.
Free o'er the Cordillera's peaks
The lordly condor stalks;
As freely through her native wilds
The Montonéra walks."

LA ZAMBULLIDÓRA."

" Nino ! tomad este anillo,
Y llevadlo á la muralla ;
Y díll á la centinéla,
Este nino va de guardia.
Vamónos, Chinas del alma !
Vamónos á zambullir.
El que zambulli se muere,
Yo tambien quiero morir !

" Huid la pompa del poblado,
Nino, huid á la savanna ;
Ali gozareis quieto
En salud hasta mañana.
Vamónos Chinas del alma !
Vamónos, á la caletá,
Para ver los guacamallos
Con fusil y bayonéta.

" Piensan luego en dispertarse
Los temblores ya dormidos ;
Volvad nino á la murallá
Salgad, ó serais perdído,
Vamónos, Chinas del alma !
Vamónos á la laguna,

A ver si en la zambullida
Encontremos una pluma,
Con que escriba la chata mia,
Las cartas de Montezuma."

Translation.

" Youth ! this magic ring receive,
   The Chinganéra's fairy spells ;
 Swift the city ramparts leave
   Nor heed the wakeful sentinel.
 Come ! beloved of my soul,
   To the depths of ocean fly ;
 Where the dark-blue billows roll,
   Fearless plunge, nor fear to die.

" To the wild savannah fly !
   Empty pomps of cities scorning
 There, beneath the vault of sky,
   Rest in safety till the morning.
 Come ! beloved of my soul,
   To the sands of ocean come ;
 There no sounds shall meet thine ear,
   Save curlew's pipe or bittern's drum.

" Hark ! the wakening earthquake's cry,
   Echoes on the startled ear :
 To the city ramparts fly,
   Youth ! for death awaits thee here.

Come! beloved of my soul,
Fly we to the desert waste;
There, where the blue waters roll,
A fairy pen, by wizards placed,
Lies for thee to write a scroll,
Such as Montezuma traced."

A FEW NOTES ON THE ARABIANS.

I HAVE heard very frequently that Arabian song is a myth that has never suffered itself to be chained to " a white prison barred with black," as I once saw a sheet of music paper described. All Arabian tradition, whether musical or otherwise, is unwritten; and memory with the Arab is the only means of preserving song or story. Harmony exists not amongst this nomad people, save in the different thickness of the tambourines, which always form the accompaniment to their singing; and there is another cause which I think may account for the diffidence that exists amongst Europeans with regard to a comprehensive study of Arabian music—the Arabs possess fourteen scales, and according to our ideas have no recognized law of rhythm or time. The following are both specimens of Arab songs, which were sent me as Arabian gypsy songs.

ARABIAN GYPSY SONG.

ARABIAN GYPSY SONG.

FINALE.

WE have wandered long enough in the wild paths of Romany Songland; already the tents are being silently folded, the camp-fires extinguished. We have passed the last of the *patrines*, heard the final notes of the gypsy's fiddle, and the highway of life lies before us. Do we regret our short divergence from the tenor of our everyday existence? have we found pleasure or *ennui* in listening for a while to the strange music of the world's Arabs? We may not have learnt much from it, nothing we can add to our crotchet-and-quaver store of musical knowledge; but we have gathered a little honey from the sweetness of Romany love-making; we have heard a few quaint tunes to the accompaniment of the guitar, the mandoline, or the violin to haunt us in our leisure moments; perchance we have gleaned a little of the gypsy wit that flashes out now from some lawless solo, now from some dangerously-wild chorus, and together with these perhaps a little more tolerance for the Romany vagabond, and through the levelling medium of the divine art to look more kindly upon a people who, though they may have "the vellum of the pedigree they claim," are not often as black as they are painted.

"To prove again that music, by the plea
  Of all men's love, has linked from sea to sea
  All shores of earth in one serene and grand symphonic land.

ERIC MACKAY.*

---

* Pablo de Sarasate.

EPILOGUE.

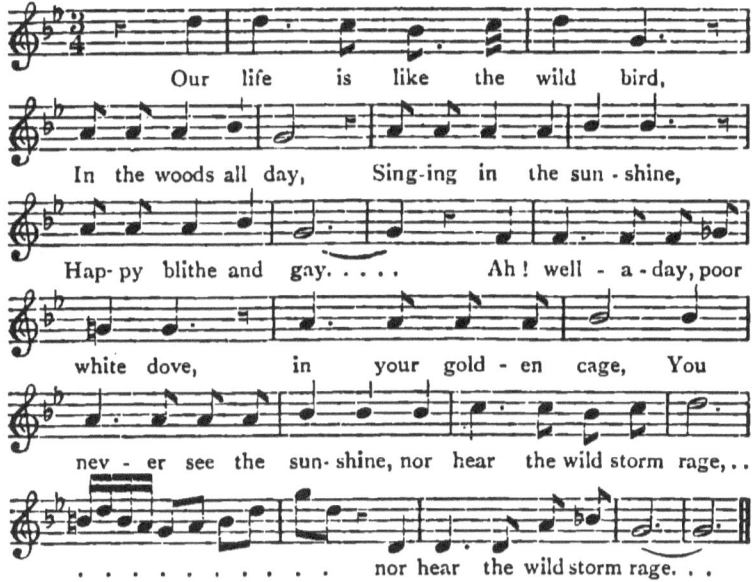

Our life is like the wild bird,
In the woods all day, Sing-ing in the sun-shine,
Hap-py blithe and gay..... Ah! well-a-day, poor
white dove, in your gold-en cage, You
nev-er see the sun-shine, nor hear the wild storm rage,..
.... nor hear the wild storm rage...

"Come then thro' the greenwoods,
   If gypsy life you'd know;
I'll lead you to the camp-fire,
   Where mirth and laughter flow.
We'll dance and sing you love-songs,
   And show you wonders deep;
And if you care to stay the night,
   On scented thyme you'll sleep."

—Cecil Traherne.

The Stott Library.

UNDER this title I am now issuing a Series of Books by the best Writers, in 32mo size, elegantly printed on toned paper, in a small but beautifully clear type. Each Volume contains an Etching as frontispiece, and the Binding is of a novel character designed by Messrs. J. BURN & Co.

The price of each Volume is Three Shillings, and any Volume can be had separately.

The Volumes already arranged for are—

ESSAYES OF MONTAIGNE. First Book. Translated by JOHN FLORIO, Introduction by JUSTIN H. M'CARTHY, M.P. Volumes 1 & 2. An Etched Portrait in each Volume. *(Now Ready.)* Volumes 3 & 4, *shortly.*

ESSAYS OF ELIA. By CHARLES LAMB, Introduction by WALTER COLLETT. Two Volumes. With Two Illustrations specially Engraved for this Edition and not before published. *(For August.)*

DE QUINCEY. A Selection of his best Works. Edited by W. H. BENNETT. Vol. 1, Confessions of an Opium Eater, &c. With Portrait. Vol. 2, Murder as one of the Fine Arts, &c. With Etching of De Quincey's Cottage.

EMERSON'S ESSAYS.

LORD BACON'S ESSAYS.

₊ Other Volumes will be duly announced.

One Hundred Copies will be issued on Large Paper.

DAVID STOTT, 370, OXFORD STREET, LONDON, W.

David Stott's Publications.

MEMOIRS OF THE MARGRAVINE OF BAIREUTH.
Translated and Edited by Her Royal Highness PRINCESS CHRISTIAN. With Portrait. Post 8vo. Price 12s.

Uniform with the above.

THE MARGRAVINE OF BAIREUTH AND VOLTAIRE.
By Dr. GEORGE HORN. Translated by H.R.H. PRINCESS CHRISTIAN. Post 8vo. Price 7s. 6d.

SAPPHO : MEMOIRS, TEXT, AND TRANSLATION.
By H.T. WHARTON, M.A. Second Edition. With Etched Portrait of Sappho, and Autotype of Fragment of Sappho's MS. Parchment, Fcap 8vo. Price 7s. 6d.

SIR PHILIP SIDNEY'S ASTROPHEL AND STELLA, WHEREIN THE EXCELLENCE OF SWEET POESY IS CONCLUDED. Edited from the Folio of 1598. By ALFRED W. POLLARD. With Portrait. Parchment, Fcap 8vo. Price 7s. 6d.

AFTER PARADISE ; or, Legends of Exile, with other Poems. By ROBERT, EARL OF LYTTON. Second Edition. Small Fcap 8vo. Price 3s. 6d.

THE EARLY LIFE OF JESUS. By Rev. STOPFORD A. BROOKE, M.A. Crown 8vo. Price 6s.

THE UNITY OF GOD AND MAN, and other Sermons. By Rev. STOPFORD A. BROOKE. Second Edition. Fcap 8vo. Price 4s.

SUNSHINE AND SHADOW. Meditations from the Writings of the Rev. STOPFORD A. BROOKE. Arranged for Daily Use. With Portrait. Second Edition. Revised. Fcap 8vo. Price 6s.

ENIGMAS OF THE SPIRITUAL LIFE. By the Rev. A. H. CRAUFURD, Author of "The Unknown God." Small 8vo. Price 6s.

THE UNKNOWN GOD. Sermons preached in London by the Rev. A. H. CRAUFURD. Second Edition. Crown 8vo. Price 6s.

TRUE RELIGION ; being a Series of Short Essays touching the intimate Relation of Religion to some Matters of Common Life. By the Rev. JOHN W. DIGGLE, Vicar of Moseley Hill, Liverpool. Crown 8vo. Price 5s.

FEDA, and other Poems, chiefly Lyrical. By RENNELL RODD. Crown 8vo. Price 6s.

POEMS IN MANY LANDS. By the same Author. Second Edition. Crown 8vo. Price 5s.

THE UNKNOWN MADONNA, and other Poems. By the same Author. With Frontispiece by W. B. RICHMOND, A.R.A. Crown 8vo, cloth. Price 5s.

DAVID STOTT'S PUBLICATIONS (continued).

FROM WEST TO EAST. By HENRY ROSE, Author of
"Three Sheiks." Crown 8vo. Price 3s. 6d.

VOLUNTARIES FOR AN EAST LONDON HOSPITAL.
Including Contributions from Lord Lytton, Austin Dobson, Andrew Lang,
R. L. Stevenson, &c., &c. Crown 8vo, cloth. Price 6s.

VERONA. By Mrs. L. ORMISTON CHANT. Fcap 8vo, cloth.
Price 5s.

CHILDREN'S FAIRY GEOGRAPHY; or, A Merry Trip
Round Europe. By Rev. FORBES E. WINSLOW, St. Leonard's-on-Sea. New
and Cheaper Edition. Eighth Thousand. Price 6s.; or with gilt sides and
gilt edges, price 7s. 6d.
"One of the most charming books ever published for young people."

FINGERS AND FORTUNE; A Guide Book to Palmistry.
By EVELINE M. FARWELL. Sixth Thousand. Fcap 8vo, cloth. Price 1s.

LOVE AND SELFISHNESS. By OSSIP SCHUBIN. Translated from the German by HARRIET F. POWELL. Crown 8vo. Price 5s.

NOW READY.

THE CHILDREN'S FAIRY HISTORY OF ENGLAND.

BY

REV. FORBES E. WINSLOW,

Author of "The Children's Fairy Geography."

4to, with 200 Illustrations, Cloth Elegant, Price 6s.

LONDON.
DAVID STOTT, 370, OXFORD STREET, W.

SAPPHO:

Memoirs, Text, and Translation.
BY
H. T. WHARTON, M.A.,
With Etched Portrait of Sappho and Autotype of Fragments of Sappho's MS.

Parchment, Fcap. 8vo.   Second Edition.   PRICE 7s. 6d.

"A pretty volume, in which Mr. H. T. Wharton has collected all the extant fragments attributed to the Greek poetess, together with a prose translation and a liberal selection of the English verse translations and imitations which have appeared since the time of Addison. . . . The chief novelty of the book is a series of translations, written expressly for it by Mr. J. A. Symonds."—*Athenæum*, June 13th, 1885.

"A valuable addition to classical literature. . . . The work cannot but prove interesting, both to scholars and to those whose ignorance of Greek debars them from a study of the Lesbian's fragmentary works in the original."—*Graphic*, June 13th, 1885.

"The little book will be treasured by all lovers of poetry, and, we may add, by all bibliophiles, for its intrinsic beauty. . . . As for Mr. Wharton's prose translations, they are characterized by admirable fidelity and self-restraint."—*The Literary World*, Boston, August 22nd, 1886.

SIR PHILIP SIDNEY'S
ASTROPHEL AND STELLA:
Wherein the Excellence of Sweet Poesy is concluded.
Edited from the Folio of 1598.
BY
ALFRED W. POLLARD.
With Portrait.   Parchment, Fcap. 8vo.   PRICE 7s. 6d.

"Edited with great care."—*Athenæum*.

"Mr. Pollard's beautiful little volume should attract many lovers of fine verse."—*Spectator*.

"A very pretty and scholarly edition of a sonnet-cycle, which well deserves all the care that editor and printer can bestow. Mr. Pollard's introduction is a capital piece of literary workmanship."—*Pall Mall Gazette*.

"A pretty, an exact, and a presentable edition of Sidney's sonnets."—*Manchester Guardian*.

"Put forth in a way that does credit to both editor and publisher."—*Literary World*.

DAVID STOTT, 370, OXFORD STREET, LONDON, W.

www.ingramcontent.com/pod-product-compliance
Lightning Source LLC
Chambersburg PA
CBHW031736230426
43669CB00007B/362